COOK
INSTANT

pi

Publications International, Ltd.

Pictured on the front cover: Balsamic Pork Roast with Potatoes *(page 118)*.

Pictured on the back cover *(clockwise from top left):* Pulled Turkey Sandwiches *(page 52),* Coconut Curry Chicken Soup *(page 26),* Shakshuka *(page 176)* and Miso Salmon *(page 146).*

Photographs on front cover and pages 45 and 119 © Shutterstock.com.

ISBN: 978-1-64030-890-9

Manufactured in China.

8 7 6 5 4 3 2 1

Note: The recipes in this book are for use in electric pressure cookers. While today's pressure cookers are built with safety features, you MUST follow the instructions which come with your pressure cooker. If you do not follow the safety instructions carefully, injury or damage may result.

Let's get social!
⊙ @Publications_International
🖪 @PublicationsInternational
www.pilcookbooks.com

CONTENTS

PRESSURE COOKING 101

Welcome to the wonderful world of electric pressure cooking! Although the current craze makes it seem like a new invention, pressure cooking has actually been around for a few hundred years. Many people grew up hearing frightening stories of pressure cooker catastrophes—exploding pots and soup on the ceiling—but those days are long gone. There have been great changes and improvements in recent years to make modern pressure cookers completely safe, quiet and easy to use.

WHAT EXACTLY IS A PRESSURE COOKER?

It's a simple concept: Liquid is heated in a heavy pot with a lid that locks and forms an airtight seal. Since the steam from the hot liquid is trapped inside and can't evaporate, the pressure increases and raises the boiling point of the contents in the pot, and these items cook faster at a higher temperature. In general, pressure cooking can reduce cooking time to about one third of the time used in conventional cooking methods—and typically the time spent on pressure cooking is hands off. (There's no peeking or stirring when food is being cooked under pressure.)

NEW AND IMPROVED

Many of the electric pressure cookers on the market today are actually multi-cookers—versatile appliances that can be a pressure cooker, slow cooker, rice cooker, steamer and even a yogurt maker. The cooking programs you'll find on the different control panels are convenient shortcuts for some foods you may prepare regularly (rice, beans, stews, etc.) which use preset times and cooking levels. But you don't need any special settings to cook great food fast. In this book we'll explore the basics of pressure cooking with recipes that use customized cooking times and pressure levels. So you'll be able to cook a wide variety of delicious dishes no matter what buttons you have on your pressure cooker.

If you're accustomed to a stovetop pressure cooker, you'll need to make a few minor adjustments when using an electric one. Electric pressure cookers regulate heat automatically, so there's no worry about adjusting the heat on a burner to maintain pressure. Also, electric pressure cookers operate at less than the conventional pressure standard of 15 pounds per square inch (psi) used by stovetop pressure cookers. Most electric pressure cookers operate at 9 to 11 psi, which means that stovetop pressure cooker recipes can be adapted to electric models by adding a little more cooking time.

PRESSURE COOKER COMPONENTS

Before beginning to cook, make sure you're familiar with the basic parts of your pressure cooker. There are some differences between brands, but they have many standard features in common. Always refer to your manual for more details and to answer questions about your specific model. (The parts are very similar but manufacturers often have different names for the same parts which can cause confusion.)

The **exterior pot** is where the electrical components are housed. It should never be immersed in water; to clean it, simply unplug the unit, wipe it with a damp cloth and dry it immediately.

The **inner pot** holds the food and fits snugly into the exterior pot. Typically made of stainless steel or aluminum with a nonstick coating, it is removable, and it can be washed by hand or some models can go in the dishwasher.

The **LED display** typically shows a time that indicates where the pressure cooker is in a particular function. For many models, the time counts down to zero from the number of minutes that were programmed. (The timing begins once the machine reaches pressure.)

The **steam release valve** (also called exhaust valve or pressure regulating valve) is on top of the lid and is used to seal the pot or release steam. To seal the pot, move the valve to the sealing or locked position; to release pressure, move the valve to the venting or open position. This valve can pop off to clean, and to make sure nothing is blocking it.

The **float valve** controls the amount of pressure inside the pressure cooker and indicates when pressure cooking is taking place—the valve rises once the contents of the pot reach working pressure; it drops down when all the pressure has been released after cooking.

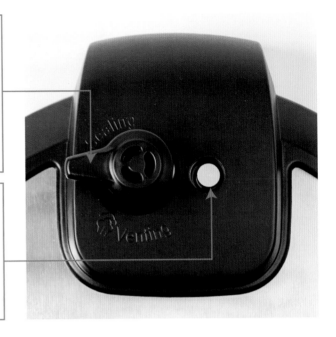

The **anti-block shield or case** is a small stainless steel cage found on the inside of the lid that prevents the pressure cooker from clogging. It can be removed for cleaning.

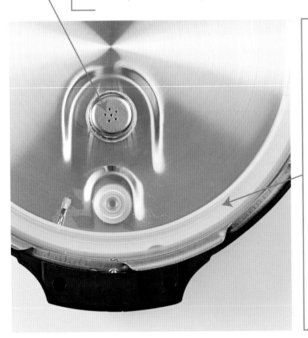

The **silicone sealing ring** (also called a gasket) underneath the lid helps create a tight seal to facilitate pressure cooking. The sealing ring has a tendency to absorb strong odors from cooking (particularly from acidic ingredients); washing it regularly with warm soapy water (or in the dishwasher if allowed) will help these odors dissipate, as will storing your pressure cooker with the lid ring side up. If you cook both sweet and savory dishes frequently, you may want to purchase an extra sealing ring (so the scent of curry or pot roast doesn't affect your rice pudding or crème brûlée). Make sure to inspect the ring before cooking—if it has any splits or cracks, it will not work properly and should be replaced.

PRESSURE COOKING BASICS

Every recipe is slightly different, but most include these basic steps. Read through the entire recipe before beginning to cook so you'll know what ingredients to add and when to add them, which pressure level to use, the cooking time and the release method.

1. Sauté or brown: Many recipes call for sautéing vegetables or browning meat at the beginning of a recipe to add flavor. (Be sure to leave the lid off in this step.)

2. Add the ingredients as the recipe directs and secure the lid, making sure it is properly locked according to the instruction manual. Turn the pressure release valve to the sealing or locked position.

3. Choose the pressure level and set the cooking time. (The default setting is usually high pressure, which is what most recipes use.) Depending on your model, the pressure cooker may start automatically or you may need to press the Start button.

4. Once the pressure cooking is complete, use the pressure release method directed by the recipe. There are three types of releases:

Natural release: Let the pressure slowly release on its own, which can take anywhere from 5 to 25 minutes (but is typically in the 10- to 15-minute range). The release time will be shorter for a pot that is less full and longer for one that is more full. When the float valve lowers, the pressure is released and you can open the lid.

Quick release: Use a towel or pot holder to manually turn the pressure release valve to the venting or open position immediately after the cooking is complete. Be sure to get out of the way of the steam, and position the pressure cooker on your countertop so the steam doesn't get expelled straight into your cabinets (or in your face). It can take up to 2 minutes to fully release all the pressure.

A combination of natural and quick release: The recipe will instruct you to let the pressure release naturally for a certain amount of time (frequently for 10 minutes), and then do a quick release as directed.

RULES OF RELEASE

Releasing pressure can be a little confusing when you first start using your pressure cooker. There's no need to worry at all about safety—you won't be able to open the lid until all the pressure has been released. And you don't need to guess which release to use since the recipes will tell you. But there are some important things to know about releasing pressure, especially when you start cooking and experimenting with the pressure cooker on your own.

Natural release is best for meats (especially larger roasts and tough cuts), foods that generate a lot of foam, such as grains, dried beans and legumes, and foods that are primarily liquid, such as soups.

Quick release is best for foods with shorter cooking times, such as vegetables and eggs, and more delicate ingredients like fish and chicken breasts. It is also used when adding additional ingredients to the pot, as is the case with some stews and vegetable dishes, and to check whether a food is done.

A **combination release** is best when a full natural release is too slow but a quick release might cause food or foam to spray through the pressure release valve.

The release method does affect the cooking time—food continues to cook during a natural release due to the residual pressure and steam in the pot. So you may discover in some dishes that you prefer a shorter cooking time with a longer release time or vice versa. (Unfortunately the two times are not in direct proportion, so it can take some trial and error to figure out what works best.)

CONTROL PANEL CONFUSION

With so many different models of pressure cookers available, it's impossible to provide specific descriptions and directions for each one. To ensure safety and the best results when cooking, read the instructions in the user's manual before beginning.

The number of programs and their names vary from one pressure cooker to another, but there are a few key settings that are common to all models and are used in the recipes in this book.

Saúté or Brown

This function is used to cook or brown ingredients in the pot before cooking them under pressure. The default cooking temperature is medium on most pressure cookers (also called "normal" on some models). Some machines allow you to raise or lower the sauté temperature; others only offer one setting. And while many electric pressure cookers have a "Saute" button, others have a "Brown" button and some have both. If your model has both, the "Brown" function cooks at a higher temperature than "Sauté." Sauté is also used to reduce and/or thicken the liquid left in the pot after cooking. Always leave the lid off when using the Sauté or Brown function.

Pressure Cooking

This control panel on your machine may have one button for high pressure and one for low pressure, or it may have a "Manual" button which allows you to choose which which pressure level you want to use. In either case, you'll need to enter the desired cooking time; some machines then start the program automatically and some require pressing a "Start" button to begin operation.

High pressure is used most often and is generally the default setting, as it allows the rapid cooking of meats, poultry, dense vegetables and frozen foods. Low pressure may be used for more delicate foods, including fish and some vegetables, and is frequently used in conjunction with a rack or steamer basket.

Cancel or Stop

This button is used to cancel a cooking program (such as when you are finished sautéing and are ready to start pressure cooking) or to turn off the pressure cooker. When the chosen time for pressure cooking is complete, some machines will automatically switch to the Keep Warm program; others require pressing the "Cancel" or "Stop" button.

Keep Warm

This function is used to keep cooked food warm until you're ready to serve, or to reheat food that has been allowed to cool.

CREAMY TOMATO SOUP

2 tablespoons olive oil

2 tablespoons butter

1 large onion, finely chopped

2 cloves garlic, minced

2 teaspoons sugar

1½ teaspoons salt

½ teaspoon dried oregano

2 cans (28 ounces each) peeled Italian plum tomatoes, undrained

Focaccia Croutons (recipe follows, optional)

½ cup whipping cream

1. Press Sauté; heat oil and butter in pot. Add onion; cook and stir 5 minutes or until softened. Add garlic, sugar, salt and oregano; cook and stir 30 seconds. Stir in tomatoes with liquid; mix well.

2. Secure lid and move pressure release valve to sealing or locked position. Cook at high pressure 8 minutes. Prepare Focaccia Croutons, if desired.

3. When cooking is complete, use natural release for 10 minutes, then release remaining pressure.

4. Use hand-held immersion blender to blend soup until smooth. Stir in cream until well blended. Serve soup with croutons.

MAKES 6 SERVINGS

FOCACCIA CROUTONS: Combine 4 cups ½-inch focaccia cubes (half of 9-ounce loaf), 1 tablespoon olive oil and ½ teaspoon black pepper in large bowl; toss to coat. Spread on large baking sheet; bake in preheated 350°F oven about 10 minutes or until bread cubes are golden brown.

MEXICAN CHICKEN AND BLACK BEAN SOUP

- **1 can (about 15 ounces) black beans, rinsed and drained**
- **1 can (about 14 ounces) fire-roasted diced tomatoes**
- **1 cup chicken broth**
- **1 cup finely chopped onion**
- **1 can (4 ounces) chopped green chiles**
- **1 tablespoon chili powder**
- **1 teaspoon ground cumin**
- **¾ teaspoon salt**
- **½ teaspoon dried oregano**
- **1 pound boneless skinless chicken thighs (about 4)**
- **1 cup frozen corn**
- **Optional toppings: sour cream, sliced avocado, shredded cheese, chopped cilantro, fried tortilla strips**

1. Combine beans, tomatoes, broth, onion, chiles, chili powder, cumin, salt and oregano in pot; mix well. Add chicken; pressing into liquid.

2. Secure lid and move pressure release valve to sealing or locked position. Cook at high pressure 10 minutes.

3. When cooking is complete, use natural release for 5 minutes, then release remaining pressure. Remove chicken to plate.

4. Press Sauté; adjust heat to low. Add corn to soup; cook about 5 minutes or until heated through. Meanwhile, shred chicken into bite-size pieces when cool enough to handle. Stir chicken into soup. Serve with desired toppings.

MAKES 4 SERVINGS

PORK AND CABBAGE SOUP

8 ounces pork loin, cut into
½-inch pieces

1 medium onion, chopped

2 slices bacon, finely chopped

1 can (about 28 ounces) whole
tomatoes, undrained, coarsely
chopped

1 teaspoon salt

1 bay leaf

¾ teaspoon dried marjoram

⅛ teaspoon black pepper

¼ medium cabbage, chopped,
divided (about 5 cups)

2 medium carrots, cut into
½-inch slices

1 cup chicken broth

2 tablespoons chopped fresh parsley

1. Press Sauté; add pork, onion and bacon to pot. Cook and stir about 5 minutes or until pork is no longer pink and onion is softened. Add tomatoes with liquid, salt, bay leaf, marjoram and pepper; cook 2 minutes, scraping up browned bits from bottom of pot. Stir in half of cabbage, carrots and broth; mix well.

2. Secure lid and move pressure release valve to sealing or locked position. Cook at high pressure 8 minutes.

3. When cooking is complete, use natural release for 10 minutes, then release remaining pressure. Remove and discard bay leaf.

4. Press Sauté; add remaining half of cabbage to pot. Cook about 3 minutes or until cabbage is wilted, stirring frequently. Stir in parsley.

MAKES 6 SERVINGS

POZOLE

- **1** tablespoon olive oil
- **1** large onion, halved then cut into ¼-inch slices
- **2** teaspoons dried oregano
- **1** clove garlic, minced
- **½** teaspoon ground cumin
- **12** ounces boneless skinless chicken thighs, cut into 1-inch strips
- **2** cans (4 ounces each) chopped green chiles
- **3** cups chicken broth
- **¼** teaspoon salt
- **1** package (10 ounces) frozen corn
- **1** can (2¼ ounces) sliced black olives, drained
- Chopped fresh cilantro (optional)
- Lime wedges (optional)

1. Press Sauté; heat oil in pot. Add onion; cook and stir about 5 minutes or until softened. Add oregano, garlic and cumin; cook and stir 1 minute. Stir in chicken and chiles until blended. Add broth and salt; mix well.

2. Secure lid and move pressure release valve to sealing or locked position. Cook at high pressure 5 minutes.

3. When cooking is complete, use natural release for 10 minutes, then release remaining pressure.

4. Press Sauté; add corn and olives to soup. Cook and stir 3 minutes or until heated through. Garnish with cilantro; serve with lime wedges, if desired.

MAKES 6 SERVINGS

RIBOLLITA (TUSCAN BREAD SOUP)

2 tablespoons olive oil

1 onion, halved and thinly sliced

2 stalks celery, diced

1 large carrot, julienned

3 cloves garlic, minced

1½ teaspoons salt

1 teaspoon Italian seasoning

1 bay leaf

¼ teaspoon black pepper

¼ teaspoon red pepper flakes (optional)

4 cups vegetable broth

1 can (28 ounces) whole tomatoes, undrained, coarsely chopped

1 can (about 15 ounces) cannellini beans, rinsed and drained

1 bunch kale, stemmed and coarsely chopped *or* 3 cups thinly sliced cabbage

8 ounces rustic Italian bread, cubed (½-inch pieces)

2 medium zucchini, thinly sliced (⅛-inch slices)

1 medium yellow squash, thinly sliced (⅛-inch slices)

Shredded Parmesan cheese (optional)

1. Press Sauté; heat oil in pot. Add onion, celery and carrot; cook and stir 5 minutes. Add garlic, salt, Italian seasoning, bay leaf, black pepper and red pepper flakes, if desired; cook and stir 1 minute. Stir in broth, tomatoes with liquid and beans; mix well.

2. Secure lid and move pressure release valve to sealing or locked position. Cook at high pressure 8 minutes. When cooking is complete, press Cancel and use quick release.

3. Add kale, bread, zucchini and yellow squash to pot. Secure lid and move pressure release valve to sealing position. Cook at high pressure 1 minute.

4. When cooking is complete, press Cancel and use quick release. Serve with cheese, if desired.

MAKES 6 TO 8 SERVINGS

NOTE: This is a great recipe to use a spiralizer if you have one. Use the spiral slicing blade to spiral the zucchini and yellow squash, then cut in half to make half moon slices. Use the thin ribbon blade to spiral the onion and carrot, and then cut into desired lengths.

TURKEY VEGETABLE RICE SOUP

6 **cups cold water**

2 **pounds turkey drumsticks (3 small)**

1 **large onion, cut into 8 wedges**

4 **tablespoons soy sauce, divided**

1 **bay leaf**

½ **teaspoon salt, divided**

½ **teaspoon black pepper, divided**

2 **carrots, sliced**

8 **ounces mushrooms, sliced**

2 **cups coarsely chopped bok choy (about 6 ounces)**

½ **cup uncooked rice**

1½ **cups fresh snow peas, cut in half crosswise**

1. Combine water, turkey, onion, 2 tablespoons soy sauce, bay leaf, ¼ teaspoon salt and ¼ teaspoon pepper in pot.

2. Secure lid and move pressure release valve to sealing or locked position. Cook at high pressure 25 minutes.

3. When cooking is complete, use natural release for 10 minutes, then release remaining pressure. Remove turkey to plate; let stand until cool enough to handle.

4. Meanwhile, add carrots, mushrooms, bok choy, rice and remaining ¼ teaspoon salt to pot; mix well. Secure lid and move pressure release valve to sealing or locked position. Cook at high pressure 4 minutes.

5. When cooking is complete, use natural release for 5 minutes, then release remaining pressure. Remove and discard bay leaf.

6. Remove turkey meat from bones; discard skin and bones. Cut turkey into bite-size pieces. Press Sauté; stir turkey, snow peas, remaining 2 tablespoons soy sauce and ¼ teaspoon pepper into soup. Cook and stir 2 to 3 minutes or until snow peas are crisp-tender.

MAKES 6 TO 8 SERVINGS

SERVING SUGGESTION: Serve with sriracha sauce for a spicy kick.

CAMPFIRE SAUSAGE AND POTATO SOUP

1 tablespoon olive oil

8 ounces kielbasa sausage, halved lengthwise, then cut crosswise into ½-inch slices

1 medium onion, diced

1 teaspoon dried oregano

1 teaspoon ground cumin

1 tablespoon tomato paste

1 large baking potato, peeled and cut into ½-inch cubes

1 can (about 15 ounces) dark red kidney beans, rinsed and drained

1 can (about 14 ounces) diced tomatoes

1 cup beef broth

1 medium green bell pepper, diced

¼ teaspoon salt

1. Press Sauté; heat oil in pot. Add sausage and onion; cook 5 minutes or until sausage is lightly browned. Add oregano and cumin; cook and stir 30 seconds. Add tomato paste; cook and stir 1 minute. Stir in potato, beans, tomatoes, broth, bell pepper and salt; mix well.

2. Secure lid and move pressure release valve to sealing or locked position. Cook at high pressure 3 minutes.

3. When cooking is complete, use natural release for 10 minutes, then release remaining pressure.

MAKES 4 TO 6 SERVINGS

SPLIT PEA SOUP WITH HAM AND ALE

1 **tablespoon olive oil**

1 **cup chopped onion**

½ **cup chopped carrot**

½ **cup chopped celery**

3 **cloves garlic, minced**

½ **teaspoon dried thyme**

1 **bottle (12 ounces) Belgian white ale**

4 **cups chicken broth**

1 **package (16 ounces) dried split peas, rinsed and sorted**

1 **pound smoked ham hocks**

1 **bay leaf**

½ **teaspoon salt**

¼ **teaspoon black pepper**

1. Press Sauté; adjust heat to low. Heat oil in pot. Add onion, carrot, celery, garlic and thyme; cook 5 minutes or until vegetables begin to soften, stirring occasionally. Add ale; cook 2 minutes, scraping up browned bits from bottom of pot. Stir in broth, split peas, ham hocks, bay leaf, salt and pepper, mix well.

2. Secure lid and move pressure release valve to sealing or locked position. Cook at high pressure 12 minutes.

3. When cooking is complete, use natural release for 10 minutes, then release remaining pressure. Remove ham hocks to cutting board; let stand until cool enough to handle. Remove and discard bay leaf. Cover pot with lid (do not lock on).

4. Remove ham from hocks; chop into bite-size pieces. Stir into soup.

MAKES 6 SERVINGS

COCONUT CURRY CHICKEN SOUP

1 can (about 14 ounces) coconut milk, divided

1½ cups chicken broth

1 cup chopped onion

2 tablespoons curry powder

1 teaspoon salt

½ teaspoon ground ginger

⅛ teaspoon ground red pepper

1½ pounds boneless skinless chicken thighs

¼ cup chopped fresh cilantro or mint

3 cups cooked rice (optional)

Lime wedges (optional)

1. Shake or stir coconut milk until well blended and smooth. Combine half of coconut milk, broth, onion, curry powder, salt, ginger and red pepper in pot; mix well. Add chicken, pressing into liquid.

2. Secure lid and move pressure release valve to sealing or locked position. Cook at high pressure 9 minutes.

3. When cooking is complete, use natural release for 10 minutes, then release remaining pressure. Remove chicken to plate; let stand until cool enough to handle.

4. Shred chicken into bite-size pieces. Press Sauté; add to pot with remaining coconut milk and cilantro. Cook 3 minutes or until heated through, stirring occasionally. Spoon rice over each serving, if desired; garnish with lime wedges.

MAKES 4 SERVINGS

ONION SOUP WITH PASTA

2 tablespoons butter

2 large onions, thinly sliced

3 cloves garlic, minced

2 teaspoons salt

½ teaspoon sugar

3 cups beef broth

½ cup uncooked small pasta stars
  or acini di pepe pasta

1 tablespoon dry sherry

  Pinch black pepper

  Grated Parmesan cheese (optional)

1. Press Sauté; melt butter in pot. Add onions and garlic; cook and stir 5 minutes or until onions are softened. Add salt and sugar; cook about 15 minutes or until onions are very soft and browned, stirring occasionally. Stir in broth and pasta; mix well.

2. Secure lid and move pressure release valve to sealing or locked position. Cook at high pressure 6 minutes.

3. When cooking is complete, press Cancel and use quick release. Stir in sherry and pepper; mix well. Serve with cheese, if desired.

MAKES 4 SERVINGS

NORTH AFRICAN CHICKEN SOUP

1 tablespoon vegetable oil

1 cup chopped onion

3 cloves garlic, minced

¾ teaspoon paprika

½ teaspoon ground cumin

½ teaspoon ground ginger

¼ teaspoon ground allspice

1¼ pounds peeled sweet potatoes, cut into 1-inch pieces (2½ cups)

2 cups chicken broth

1 can (about 14 ounces) whole tomatoes, undrained, cut up or crushed with hands

12 ounces boneless skinless chicken thighs, cut into 1-inch pieces

½ teaspoon salt

¼ to ½ teaspoon black pepper

Hot pepper sauce and lime juice (optional)

1. Press Sauté; heat oil in pot. Add onion; cook and stir 3 minutes or until softened. Add garlic; cook and stir 30 seconds. Add paprika, cumin, ginger and allspice; cook and stir 30 seconds. Stir in sweet potatoes, broth, tomatoes with liquid, chicken and salt; mix well.

2. Secure lid and move pressure release valve to sealing or locked position. Cook at high pressure 5 minutes.

3. When cooking is complete, use natural release for 10 minutes, then release remaining pressure. Stir in black pepper to taste. Serve with hot pepper sauce and lime juice, if desired.

MAKES 4 TO 6 SERVINGS

CARROT AND CORIANDER SOUP

¼ cup (½ stick) butter

4 cups grated carrots (about 1 pound)

1 cup finely chopped onion

2 cups vegetable broth

1½ teaspoons ground coriander

1½ teaspoons ground cumin

1 teaspoon salt

1 clove garlic, minced

2 tablespoons finely chopped fresh cilantro

1 tablespoon lemon juice

⅛ teaspoon black pepper

1. Press Sauté; melt butter in pot. Add carrots and onion; cook and stir 5 minutes or until softened. Stir in broth, coriander, cumin, salt and garlic; mix well.

2. Secure lid and move pressure release valve to sealing or locked position. Cook at high pressure 8 minutes.

3. When cooking is complete, use natural release for 5 minutes, then release remaining pressure.

4. Use hand-held immersion blender to blend soup until smooth. Stir in cilantro, lemon juice and pepper until well blended.

MAKES 4 SERVINGS

BEEF FAJITA SOUP

1 **pound beef stew meat, cut into 1-inch pieces**

1 **can (about 15 ounces) pinto beans, rinsed and drained**

1 **can (about 15 ounces) black beans, rinsed and drained**

1 **can (about 14 ounces) beef broth**

1 **can (about 10 ounces) diced tomatoes with green chiles**

1 **green bell pepper, cut into ½-inch slices**

1 **red bell pepper, cut into ½-inch slices**

1 **onion, cut into ¼-inch slices**

2 **teaspoons ground cumin**

1 **teaspoon seasoned salt**

½ **teaspoon black pepper**

Optional toppings: sour cream, shredded Monterey Jack or Cheddar cheese, chopped olives

1. Combine beef, beans, broth, tomatoes, bell peppers, onion, cumin, seasoned salt and black pepper in pot; mix well.

2. Secure lid and move pressure release valve to sealing or locked position. Cook at high pressure 25 minutes.

3. When cooking is complete, use natural release for 10 minutes, then release remaining pressure. Serve with desired toppings.

MAKES 8 SERVINGS

SPEEDY MINESTRONE

1 tablespoon olive oil

1 medium onion, chopped

3 medium carrots, chopped

3 stalks celery, chopped

2 cloves garlic, minced

1½ teaspoons salt

1 teaspoon Italian seasoning

¼ teaspoon black pepper

⅛ teaspoon red pepper flakes

4 cups vegetable broth

2 russet potatoes (about 6 ounces each), peeled and cut into ½-inch pieces

2 cans (about 15 ounces each) cannellini beans, rinsed and drained

1 can (about 14 ounces) diced tomatoes

1 bunch kale, stemmed and chopped (about 6 cups)

Shredded Parmesan cheese (optional)

1. Press Sauté; heat oil in pot. Add onion, carrots, celery and garlic; cook and stir 5 minutes or until vegetables are softened. Add salt, Italian seasoning, black pepper and red pepper flakes; cook and stir 1 minute. Stir in broth, potatoes, beans and tomatoes; mix well.

2. Secure lid and move pressure release valve to sealing or locked position. Cook at high pressure 3 minutes.

3. When cooking is complete, press Cancel and use quick release. Stir in kale. Secure lid and move pressure release valve to sealing position. Cook at high pressure 2 minutes.

4. When cooking is complete, use natural release for 5 minutes, then release remaining pressure. Serve with cheese, if desired.

MAKES 6 TO 8 SERVINGS

THAI PUMPKIN CHICKEN SOUP

1 tablespoon vegetable oil

1 pound boneless skinless chicken breasts, cut into 1-inch pieces

1 white onion, thinly sliced

2 stalks celery, diced

2 carrots, diced

1 tablespoon minced garlic

1 tablespoon minced fresh ginger

½ teaspoon salt

¼ to ½ teaspoon red pepper flakes

2 cups chicken broth

1 cup canned pumpkin

½ cup creamy peanut butter

½ cup minced fresh cilantro, divided

2 tablespoons rice vinegar

1 tablespoon cornstarch

2 tablespoons lime juice

Hot cooked jasmine or basmati rice

2 green onions, minced

½ cup roasted unsalted peanuts, coarsely chopped

Lime wedges (optional)

1. Press Sauté; heat oil in pot. Add chicken; cook and stir 5 minutes or until no longer pink. Add onion, celery, carrots, garlic, ginger, salt and red pepper flakes to pot; cook and stir 5 minutes or until vegetables begin to soften. Stir in broth, pumpkin, peanut butter, ¼ cup cilantro and vinegar; mix well.

2. Secure lid and move pressure release valve to sealing or locked position. Cook at high pressure 5 minutes.

3. When cooking is complete, use natural release for 10 minutes, then release remaining pressure.

4. Stir ¼ cup hot soup into cornstarch in small bowl until smooth. Press Sauté; add cornstarch mixture to pot. Cook and stir 2 to 3 minutes or until soup thickens. Stir in lime juice. Serve soup with rice, remaining ¼ cup cilantro, green onions, peanuts and lime wedges, if desired.

MAKES 6 SERVINGS

LENTIL RICE SOUP

1 tablespoon olive oil

1 onion, finely chopped

2 carrots, finely chopped

2 stalks celery, finely chopped

2 teaspoons minced garlic

1 teaspoon salt

1 teaspoon herbes de Provence

⅛ teaspoon black pepper

6 cups vegetable broth

1 cup dried lentils, rinsed and sorted

¼ cup uncooked rice, rinsed well

¼ cup chopped fresh parsley

Sour cream (optional)

1. Press Sauté; heat oil in pot. Add onion, carrots, celery and garlic; cook and stir 5 minutes or until vegetables are softened. Add salt, herbes de Provence and pepper; cook and stir 30 seconds. Stir in broth, lentils and rice; mix well.

2. Secure lid and move pressure release valve to sealing or locked position. Cook at high pressure 10 minutes.

3. When cooking is complete, use natural release for 10 minutes, then release remaining pressure. Stir in parsley. Top with sour cream, if desired.

MAKES 4 TO 6 SERVINGS

BUFFALO CHICKEN WINGS

- **3 pounds chicken wings, tips discarded, separated at joints**
- **1 teaspoon garlic powder**
- **1 teaspoon salt, divided**
- **½ cup water**
- **⅓ cup butter**
- **⅔ cup hot pepper sauce**
- **1½ teaspoons Worcestershire sauce**
- **1 teaspoon packed brown sugar**
- **Ranch dressing (optional)**
- **Celery sticks (optional)**

1. Season wings with garlic powder and ¾ teaspoon salt. Pour water into pot. Place rack in pot; place wings on rack (or use steamer basket to hold wings).

2. Secure lid and move pressure release valve to sealing or locked position. Cook at high pressure 5 minutes.

3. Meanwhile, preheat broiler. Line baking sheet with foil. Microwave butter in large microwavable bowl until melted. Stir in hot pepper sauce, Worcestershire sauce, brown sugar and remaining ¼ teaspoon salt until well blended.

4. When cooking is complete, press Cancel and use quick release. Pat wings dry with paper towels; add to bowl of sauce and toss well to coat. Spread wings in single layer on prepared baking sheet. (Reserve sauce left in bowl.)

5. Broil about 6 minutes or until browned. Turn and brush with sauce; broil 4 to 5 minutes or until browned. Return wings to bowl with sauce; toss to coat. Serve wings with ranch dressing and celery, if desired.

MAKES 4 TO 6 SERVINGS

COQ AU VIN

4 slices thick-cut bacon, cut into
½-inch pieces

8 bone-in skinless chicken thighs
(3½ to 4 pounds)

1 teaspoon salt

½ teaspoon black pepper

1 package (8 to 10 ounces) cremini
or white mushrooms, quartered

3 medium carrots, cut into
1½-inch pieces

1 tablespoon tomato paste

2 cloves garlic, minced

10 sprigs fresh thyme

1½ cups dry red wine

8 ounces frozen pearl onions (about
1½ cups), divided

1 bay leaf

1 tablespoon butter, softened

1 tablespoon all-purpose flour

Chopped fresh parsley (optional)

1. Press Sauté; cook bacon in pot until crisp. Remove to paper towel-lined plate.

2. Season both sides of chicken with 1 teaspoon salt and ½ teaspoon pepper. Add chicken to drippings in pot in two batches; cook 3 to 4 minutes per side or until browned. Remove to plate.

3. Add mushrooms and carrots to pot; cook about 6 minutes or until mushrooms have given off their liquid and begin to brown, stirring occasionally and scraping up browned bits from bottom of pot. Add tomato paste, garlic and thyme; cook and stir 2 minutes. Stir in wine; cook about 10 minutes or until reduced by half. Return chicken to pot with half of onions, half of bacon and bay leaf.

4. Secure lid and move pressure release valve to sealing or locked position. Cook at high pressure 14 minutes. Meanwhile, mix butter and flour in small bowl until well blended.

5. When cooking is complete, press Cancel and use quick release. Remove chicken and vegetables to platter with slotted spoon. Remove and discard thyme sprigs and bay leaf.

6. Press Sauté; add butter mixture and remaining half of onions to pot. Cook and stir 2 to 3 minutes or until sauce thickens. Season with additional salt and pepper, if desired. Pour sauce over chicken and vegetables. Garnish with reserved bacon and parsley, if desired.

MAKES 4 TO 6 SERVINGS

PESTO TURKEY MEATBALLS

1 pound ground turkey

⅓ **cup prepared pesto**

⅓ **cup grated Parmesan cheese, plus additional for garnish**

¼ **cup panko bread crumbs**

1 egg

2 green onions, finely chopped

½ **teaspoon salt, divided**

2 tablespoons olive oil

2 cloves garlic, minced

⅛ **teaspoon red pepper flakes**

1 can (28 ounces) whole tomatoes, undrained, crushed with hands or coarsely chopped

1 tablespoon tomato paste

Hot cooked pasta (optional)

Chopped fresh basil (optional)

1. Combine turkey, pesto, ⅓ cup cheese, panko, egg, green onions and ¼ teaspoon salt in medium bowl; mix well. Shape mixture into 24 (1¼-inch) meatballs. Refrigerate meatballs while preparing sauce.

2. Press Sauté; heat oil in pot. Add garlic and red pepper flakes; cook and stir 1 minute. Add tomatoes with liquid, tomato paste and remaining ¼ teaspoon salt; cook 3 minutes or until sauce begins to simmer, stirring occasionally.

3. Remove about 1 cup sauce from pot. Arrange meatballs in single layer in pot; pour reserved sauce over meatballs.

4. Secure lid and move pressure release valve to sealing or locked position. Cook on high pressure 10 minutes.

5. When cooking is complete, use natural release for 10 minutes, then release remaining pressure. If sauce is too thin, press Sauté and cook 5 minutes or until sauce thickens, stirring frequently. Serve over pasta, if desired. Garnish with additional cheese and basil.

MAKES 4 SERVINGS

AUTUMN CHICKEN AND VEGETABLES

3 to 4 pounds bone-in chicken thighs

½ **teaspoon salt**

½ **teaspoon black pepper**

½ **cup all-purpose flour**

2 **tablespoons olive oil**

½ **cup apple cider or juice**

¼ **cup chicken broth**

1 **teaspoon dried thyme**

1 **small butternut squash, cut into ¾-inch pieces (about 4 cups)**

1 **bulb fennel, thinly sliced**

½ **cup walnuts (optional)**

2 **tablespoons chopped fresh basil (optional)**

1. Season chicken with salt and pepper; coat lightly with flour. Press Sauté; heat oil in pot. Add chicken in two batches; cook about 5 minutes per side or until browned. Remove to plate. Stir in cider, broth and thyme; cook 1 minute, scraping up browned bits from bottom of pot. Return chicken to pot, pressing into liquid.

2. Secure lid and move pressure release valve to sealing or locked position. Cook at high pressure 6 minutes.

3. When cooking is complete, press Cancel and use quick release.

4. Add squash and fennel to pot. Secure lid and move pressure release valve to sealing or locked position. Cook at high pressure 3 minutes.

5. When cooking is complete, press Cancel and use quick release. Remove chicken and vegetables to plate; tent with foil.

6. Press Sauté; cook about 5 minutes or until sauce is reduced by one third and thickens slightly. Serve sauce with chicken and vegetables; sprinkle with walnuts and basil, if desired.

MAKES 6 SERVINGS

INDIAN-STYLE APRICOT CHICKEN

2½ **pounds bone-in skinless chicken thighs (about 6)**

½ **teaspoon salt**

¼ **teaspoon black pepper**

1 **tablespoon vegetable oil**

1 **large onion, chopped**

½ **cup chicken broth, divided**

1 **tablespoon grated fresh ginger**

2 **cloves garlic, minced**

½ **teaspoon ground cinnamon**

⅛ **teaspoon ground allspice**

1 **can (about 14 ounces) diced tomatoes**

1 **package (8 ounces) dried apricots**

Pinch saffron threads (optional)

Hot cooked basmati rice (optional)

Chopped fresh Italian parsley (optional)

1. Season chicken with ½ teaspoon salt and ¼ teaspoon pepper. Press Sauté; heat oil in pot. Add chicken in two batches; cook about 4 minutes per side or until browned. Remove to plate.

2. Add onion and 2 tablespoons broth to pot; cook 5 minutes or until onion is translucent, scraping up browned bits from bottom of pot. Add ginger, garlic, cinnamon and allspice; cook and stir 30 seconds or until fragrant. Stir in tomatoes, apricots, remaining broth and saffron, if desired; mix well. Return chicken to pot, pressing into liquid.

3. Secure lid and move pressure release valve to sealing or locked position. Cook at high pressure 11 minutes.

4. When cooking is complete, press Cancel and use quick release. Season with additional salt and pepper. Serve with rice, if desired. Garnish with parsley.

MAKES 4 TO 6 SERVINGS

TIP: To remove chicken skin easily, grasp skin with paper towel and pull away.

PULLED TURKEY SANDWICHES

1 tablespoon vegetable oil

1 small red onion, finely chopped

1 can (8 ounces) tomato sauce

¼ cup ketchup

2 tablespoons packed brown sugar

1 tablespoon cider vinegar

2 teaspoons Worcestershire sauce

1 teaspoon Dijon mustard

¼ teaspoon salt

¼ teaspoon chipotle chili powder

1½ pounds turkey tenderloins (2 small), each cut in half

4 sandwich rolls or buns

1. Press Sauté; heat oil in pot. Add onion; cook and stir 3 minutes or until softened. Add tomato sauce, ketchup, brown sugar, vinegar, Worcestershire sauce, mustard, salt and chili powder; mix well. Cook and stir about 5 minutes or until sauce is reduced and thickened.

2. Add turkey; turn to coat all sides with sauce. Secure lid and move pressure release valve to sealing or locked position. Cook at high pressure 20 minutes.

3. When cooking is complete, use natural release for 10 minutes, then release remaining pressure. Remove turkey to plate; set aside until cool enough to handle.

4. Press Sauté; adjust heat to low. Cook 8 to 10 minutes or until sauce is reduced and thickens slightly.

5. Shred turkey into bite-size pieces; add to sauce and stir until well blended. Serve on rolls.

MAKES 4 SANDWICHES

TIP: The turkey filling freezes well, so try doubling the recipe and freezing the leftovers. Before serving, simply thaw the filling in the refrigerator and reheat in the microwave.

ARTICHOKE DIJON CHICKEN THIGHS

1 jar (12 ounces) quartered marinated artichoke hearts, undrained

⅓ cup Dijon mustard

2 tablespoons minced garlic

½ teaspoon dried tarragon

¼ teaspoon salt

2½ pounds bone-in skinless chicken thighs (about 6)

1½ cups thickly sliced mushrooms

1 cup chopped onion

2 tablespoons water

1 tablespoon all-purpose flour

¼ cup chopped fresh parsley

Hot cooked pasta (optional)

1. Drain artichokes, reserving ½ cup marinade. (Discard remaining marinade.) Combine reserved marinade, mustard, garlic, tarragon and salt in pot; mix well. Add chicken, mushrooms and onion; stir to coat.

2. Secure lid and move pressure release valve to sealing or locked position. Cook at high pressure 11 minutes.

3. When cooking is complete, use natural release for 10 minutes, then release remaining pressure. Remove chicken to plate; tent with foil.

4. Press Sauté; add artichokes to pot. Cook about 5 minutes or until artichokes are heated through and sauce is reduced by half, stirring occasionally.

5. Stir water into flour in small bowl until smooth. Add to sauce; cook and stir 1 minute or until sauce thickens. Stir in parsley. Serve chicken and sauce over pasta, if desired.

MAKES 4 TO 6 SERVINGS

BUTTER CHICKEN

2 tablespoons butter

1 onion, chopped

4 cloves garlic, minced

1 teaspoon minced fresh ginger

1 teaspoon ground turmeric

1 teaspoon ground coriander

1 teaspoon garam masala

1 teaspoon ground cumin

½ teaspoon ground red pepper

½ teaspoon paprika

1 can (about 14 ounces) diced tomatoes

¾ teaspoon salt

2 pounds boneless skinless chicken breasts, cut into 2-inch pieces

½ cup whipping cream

Chopped fresh cilantro

Hot cooked rice (optional)

1. Press Sauté; melt butter in pot. Add onion; cook and stir about 3 minutes or until onion begins to turn golden. Add garlic and ginger; cook and stir 1 minute. Add turmeric, coriander, garam masala, cumin, red pepper and paprika; cook and stir 30 seconds. Add tomatoes and salt; cook and stir 2 minutes. Stir in chicken; mix well.

2. Secure lid and move pressure release valve to sealing or locked position. Cook on high pressure 8 minutes.

3. When cooking is complete, use natural release for 10 minutes, then release remaining pressure.

4. Press Sauté; adjust heat to low. Stir in cream; cook 5 minutes or until heated through. Sprinkle with cilantro; serve with rice, if desired.

MAKES 4 TO 6 SERVINGS

CHILI WAGON WHEEL PASTA

1 tablespoon olive oil

1 pound ground turkey

1 cup chopped onion

1 green bell pepper, chopped

2 teaspoons salt

2 teaspoons chili powder

½ teaspoon dried oregano

½ teaspoon black pepper

¼ teaspoon ground allspice

1 can (about 14 ounces) diced tomatoes

1 can (8 ounces) tomato sauce

½ cup water

8 ounces uncooked mini wagon wheel pasta

1 cup (4 ounces) shredded Cheddar cheese

1. Press Sauté; heat oil in pot. Add turkey; cook 5 minutes or until cooked through, stirring frequently. Add onion and bell pepper; cook and stir 3 minutes or until softened. Add salt, chili powder, oregano, black pepper and allspice; cook and stir 30 seconds. Stir in tomatoes, tomato sauce and water; mix well. Stir in pasta.

2. Secure lid and move pressure release valve to sealing or locked position. Cook at high pressure 4 minutes.

3. When cooking is complete, press Cancel and use quick release. Stir in cheese.

MAKES 4 SERVINGS

CURRIED CHICKEN AND WINTER VEGETABLE STEW

1 tablespoon vegetable oil

1 medium onion, chopped

1 tablespoon curry powder

1 clove garlic, minced

1 pound boneless skinless chicken breasts, cut into ½-inch pieces

1 can (about 14 ounces) diced tomatoes

1 cup chicken broth

2 medium turnips, cut into 1-inch pieces

2 medium carrots, cut into 1-inch slices

½ cup raisins (optional)

¼ cup tomato paste

1 teaspoon salt

⅛ teaspoon ground red pepper

1. Press Sauté; adjust heat to low. Heat oil in pot. Add onion; cook and stir 3 minutes or until softened. Add curry powder and garlic; cook and stir 1 minute. Stir in chicken, tomatoes, broth, turnips, carrots, raisins, if desired, tomato paste, salt and red pepper; mix well.

2. Secure lid and move pressure release valve to sealing or locked position. Cook at high pressure 5 minutes.

3. When cooking is complete, use natural release for 5 minutes, then release remaining pressure.

MAKES 4 TO 6 SERVINGS

SERVING SUGGESTION: Serve with couscous or brown rice.

LEMON ROSEMARY CHICKEN AND POTATOES

4 **bone-in skinless chicken breasts (about 8 ounces each)**

2 **pounds small red potatoes, cut into halves or quarters (1½-inch pieces)**

1 **large onion, cut into 2-inch pieces**

½ **cup lemon juice**

6 **tablespoons olive oil**

6 **cloves garlic, minced**

2 **tablespoons plus 1 teaspoon finely chopped fresh rosemary leaves *or* 2¼ teaspoons dried rosemary**

2 **teaspoons grated lemon peel**

1½ **teaspoons salt**

½ **teaspoon black pepper**

1 **tablespoon vegetable oil**

½ **cup chicken broth**

1. Place chicken in large resealable food storage bag. Place potatoes and onion in another resealable bag. Combine lemon juice, olive oil, garlic, rosemary, lemon peel, 1½ teaspoons salt and pepper in small bowl; mix well. Pour half of marinade (about 6 tablespoons) over chicken; pour remaining marinade over potatoes and onion. Seal bags and turn to coat. Refrigerate 2 hours or overnight.

2. Remove chicken from marinade; discard marinade. Press Sauté; heat vegetable oil in pot. Add chicken in two batches; cook about 5 minutes per side or until browned. Remove to plate.

3. Remove potatoes and onion from marinade; reserve marinade. Add vegetables to pot; cook and stir 3 minutes, scraping up browned bits from bottom of pot. Arrange chicken on top of vegetables; pour reserved marinade and broth over chicken.

4. Secure lid and move pressure release valve to sealing or locked position. Cook at high pressure 9 minutes.

5. When cooking is complete, press Cancel and use quick release. Remove chicken and vegetables to platter; tent with foil.

6. Skim excess fat from surface of cooking liquid. Press Sauté; cook about 5 minutes or until sauce is slightly reduced. Season vegetables with additional salt, if desired. Serve sauce over chicken and vegetables.

MAKES 4 SERVINGS

MU SHU TURKEY

1 jar (about 7 ounces) plum sauce, divided

¼ cup orange juice

¼ cup finely chopped onion

1 tablespoon minced fresh ginger

¼ teaspoon salt

¼ teaspoon ground cinnamon

1 pound boneless turkey breast, cut into thin strips

6 (7-inch) flour tortillas

3 cups coleslaw mix

1. Combine ⅓ cup plum sauce, orange juice, onion, ginger, salt and cinnamon in pot; mix well. Add turkey, stir to coat.

2. Secure lid and move pressure release valve to sealing or locked position. Cook at high pressure 4 minutes.

3. When cooking is complete, press Cancel or Stop and use quick release.

4. Press Sauté; cook 2 to 3 minutes or until sauce is reduced and thickens slightly.

5. Spread remaining jarred plum sauce over tortillas; top with turkey and coleslaw mix. Fold bottom edge of tortillas over filling; fold in sides and roll up to completely enclose filling. Serve with remaining cooking sauce for dipping.

MAKES 6 SERVINGS

QUICK CHICKEN AND BEAN STEW

1 **pound boneless skinless chicken thighs, cut into 1-inch pieces**

1 **can (about 15 ounces) Great Northern beans, rinsed and drained**

1 **can (about 15 ounces) black beans, rinsed and drained**

1 **can (about 14 ounces) crushed tomatoes (preferably fire-roasted)**

1 **onion, chopped**

⅓ **cup chicken broth**

Juice of 1 large orange (about ⅓ cup)

1 **canned chipotle pepper in adobo sauce, minced**

1 **teaspoon salt**

1 **teaspoon ground cumin**

1 **bay leaf**

Fresh cilantro sprigs (optional)

1. Combine chicken, beans, tomatoes, onion, broth, orange juice, chipotle pepper, salt, cumin and bay leaf in pot; mix well.

2. Secure lid and move pressure release valve to sealing or locked position. Cook at high pressure 6 minutes.

3. When cooking is complete, use natural release for 5 minutes, then release remaining pressure.

4. Press Sauté; cook 3 to 5 minutes or until stew thickens, stirring frequently. Remove and discard bay leaf. Garnish with cilantro.

MAKES 4 TO 6 SERVINGS

HERB LEMON TURKEY BREAST

½ **cup lemon juice**

½ **cup dry white wine**

4 **cloves garlic, minced**

1 **teaspoon salt**

½ **teaspoon dried parsley flakes**

½ **teaspoon dried tarragon**

½ **teaspoon dried rosemary**

¼ **teaspoon ground sage**

¼ **teaspoon black pepper**

1 **boneless turkey breast (about 3 pounds)**

Fresh rosemary sprigs and lemon slices (optional)

1. Combine lemon juice, wine, garlic, salt, parsley flakes, tarragon, dried rosemary, sage and pepper in measuring cup or small bowl; mix well.

2. Place turkey breast in pot; pour juice mixture over turkey, turning to coat. (Turkey should be right side up for cooking.)

3. Secure lid and move pressure release valve to sealing or locked position. Cook at high pressure 30 minutes.

4. When cooking is complete, use natural release for 10 minutes, then release remaining pressure. Remove turkey to cutting board; tent with foil. Let stand 10 minutes before slicing.

5. Use cooking liquid as sauce, if desired, or thicken liquid with flour (see Tip). Garnish as desired.

MAKES 4 SERVINGS

TIP: **If desired, prepare gravy with cooking liquid after removing turkey from pot. Place ¼ cup all-purpose flour in small bowl; stir in ½ cup cooking liquid until smooth. Press Sauté; add flour mixture to pot. Cook 5 minutes or until gravy thickens, stirring frequently.**

WHITE CHICKEN CHILI

1 tablespoon vegetable oil

1½ pounds boneless skinless chicken breasts

2 medium onions, chopped

1 can (4 ounces) diced green chiles

1 tablespoon minced garlic

2 teaspoons ground cumin

1 teaspoon salt

1 teaspoon dried oregano

¼ teaspoon black pepper

¼ teaspoon ground red pepper

1½ cups chicken broth

2 cans (about 15 ounces each) Great Northern beans, rinsed and drained

¼ cup chopped fresh cilantro

1. Press Sauté; heat oil in pot. Add chicken; cook about 3 minutes per side or until browned. Remove to plate.

2. Add onions and chiles to pot; cook and stir 3 minutes. Add garlic, cumin, salt, oregano, black pepper and red pepper; cook and stir 1 minute. Stir in broth, scraping up browned bits from bottom of pot. Stir in beans; mix well. Return chicken to pot, pressing into liquid.

3. Secure lid and move pressure release valve to sealing or locked position. Cook at high pressure 7 minutes.

4. When cooking is complete, press Cancel and use quick release. Remove chicken to clean plate; set aside until cool enough to handle.

5. Shred chicken into bite-size pieces; return to pot. Press Sauté; cook 2 to 3 minutes or until chili thickens slightly. Sprinkle with cilantro.

MAKES 6 SERVINGS

TURKEY STROGANOFF

1 tablespoon olive oil

4 cups sliced mushrooms

2 stalks celery, sliced

2 medium shallots *or* ½ small onion, minced

2 turkey tenderloins (about 5 ounces each), cut into 1-inch pieces

¼ cup chicken broth

1½ tablespoons Worcestershire sauce

¾ teaspoon salt

½ teaspoon dried thyme

¼ teaspoon black pepper

½ cup sour cream

1 tablespoon all-purpose flour

Hot cooked egg noodles

1. Press Sauté; heat oil in pot. Add mushrooms, celery and shallots; cook and stir 5 minutes or until vegetables are softened. Add turkey, broth, Worcestershire sauce, salt, thyme and pepper; mix well.

2. Secure lid and move pressure release valve to sealing or locked position. Cook at high pressure 6 minutes.

3. When cooking is complete, use natural release for 5 minutes, then release remaining pressure.

4. Combine sour cream and flour in small bowl; stir in ¼ cup hot cooking liquid from pot until smooth. Press Sauté; add sour cream mixture to pot. Cook and stir 3 minutes or until sauce thickens. Serve over noodles.

MAKES 4 SERVINGS

HOISIN BARBECUE CHICKEN SLIDERS

⅔ **cup hoisin sauce**

⅓ **cup barbecue sauce**

1 **tablespoon soy sauce**

¼ **teaspoon red pepper flakes**

3 **to 3½ pounds boneless skinless chicken thighs**

2 **tablespoons water**

1 **tablespoon cornstarch**

16 **dinner rolls or Hawaiian sweet rolls, split**

½ **medium red onion, finely chopped**

   Sliced pickles (optional)

1. Combine hoisin sauce, barbecue sauce, soy sauce and red pepper flakes in pot; mix well. Add chicken; stir to coat.

2. Secure lid and move pressure release valve to sealing or locked position. Cook at high pressure 8 minutes.

3. When cooking is complete, use natural release for 5 minutes, then release remaining pressure. Remove chicken to plate; let stand until cool enough to handle. Shred chicken into bite-size pieces.

4. Stir water into cornstarch in small bowl until smooth. Press Sauté; add cornstarch mixture to pot. Cook and stir about 2 minutes or until sauce thickens. Return chicken to pot; mix well. Spoon about ¼ cup chicken mixture onto each roll; serve with onion and pickles, if desired.

MAKES 16 SLIDERS

EASY MEATBALLS

1 pound ground beef

1 egg, beaten

3 tablespoons Italian-seasoned
dry bread crumbs

1 clove garlic, minced

1 teaspoon dried oregano

¾ teaspoon salt

¼ teaspoon black pepper

⅛ teaspoon ground red pepper

3 cups marinara or tomato-basil
pasta sauce

Hot cooked spaghetti

Chopped fresh basil (optional)

Grated Parmesan cheese (optional)

1. Combine beef, egg, bread crumbs, garlic, oregano, salt, black pepper and red pepper in medium bowl; mix gently. Shape into 16 (1½-inch) meatballs.

2. Pour pasta sauce into pot. Add meatballs to sauce; turn to coat and submerge meatballs in sauce.

3. Secure lid and move pressure release valve to sealing or locked position. Cook at high pressure 8 minutes.

4. When cooking is complete, press Cancel and use quick release. Serve meatballs and sauce over spaghetti; top with basil and cheese, if desired.

MAKES 4 SERVINGS

CREOLE-SPICED POT ROAST

2 tablespoons Creole or Cajun seasoning

1 boneless beef chuck roast (3 pounds), cut in half

1 tablespoon vegetable oil

1 medium onion, chopped

1 can (about 14 ounces) diced tomatoes, drained

1 can (about 14 ounces) diced tomatoes with green chiles, drained

2 tablespoons hot pepper sauce

1 teaspoon sugar

½ teaspoon black pepper

1 cup chopped rutabaga

1 cup chopped mushrooms

1 cup chopped turnip

1 cup chopped parsnip

1 cup chopped green bell pepper

1 cup green beans

1 cup sliced carrots

1 cup corn

1. Rub Creole seasoning into all sides of beef. Press Sauté; heat oil in pot. Add beef; cook about 10 minutes or until browned on all sides. Add onion to pot during last few minutes of cooking, stirring until softened. Add tomatoes, hot pepper sauce, sugar and black pepper; mix well.

2. Secure lid and move pressure release valve to sealing or locked position. Cook at high pressure 65 minutes.

3. When cooking is complete, press Cancel and use quick release. Add rutabaga, mushrooms, turnip, parsnip, bell pepper, green beans, carrots and corn to pot, pressing vegetables down into liquid.

4. Secure lid and move pressure release valve to sealing or locked position. Cook at high pressure 10 minutes.

5. When cooking is complete, press Cancel and use quick release.

MAKES 6 SERVINGS

TACO SALAD

CHILI

- 1 **pound ground beef**
- 1 **medium onion, chopped**
- 1 **stalk celery, chopped**
- 2 **medium tomatoes, chopped**
- 1 **jalapeño pepper,* finely chopped**
- 1½ **teaspoons chili powder**
- 1 **teaspoon salt**
- 1 **teaspoon ground cumin**
- ½ **teaspoon black pepper**
- 1 **can (15 ounces) tomato sauce**
- 1 **can (about 15 ounces) kidney beans, rinsed and drained**
- 1 **can (about 15 ounces) pinto beans, rinsed and drained**
- ½ **cup water**

SALAD

- 8 **cups chopped romaine lettuce (large pieces)**
- 2 **cups diced fresh tomatoes**
- 2 **cups small tortilla chips**

Optional toppings: salsa, sour cream, shredded Cheddar cheese

*Jalapeño peppers can sting and irritate the skin, so wear rubber gloves when handling peppers and do not touch your eyes.

1. Press Sauté; add beef to pot. Cook about 8 minutes or until browned, stirring frequently. Drain off fat and excess liquid. Add onion and celery to pot; cook and stir 3 minutes.

2. Add tomatoes, jalapeño, chili powder, salt, cumin and black pepper; cook and stir 1 minute. Stir in tomato sauce, beans and water; mix well.

3. Secure lid and move pressure release valve to sealing or locked position. Cook at high pressure 20 minutes.

4. When cooking is complete, use natural release for 10 minutes, then release remaining pressure.

5. For each salad, combine 2 cups lettuce and ½ cup diced tomatoes in individual bowl. Top with tortilla chips, chili, salsa, sour cream and cheese, if desired. (Recipe makes more chili than needed for salads; reserve remaining chili for another use.)

MAKES 4 SERVINGS

CLASSIC BEEF STEW

¼ cup all-purpose flour

1½ teaspoons salt, divided

2½ pounds cubed beef stew meat

2 tablespoons olive oil, divided

1 cup beef broth

1 medium onion, chopped

1 ounce dried oyster mushrooms, chopped

2 teaspoons garlic powder

1 teaspoon dried basil

1 teaspoon dried oregano

½ teaspoon dried rosemary

½ teaspoon dried marjoram

½ teaspoon dried sage

½ teaspoon dried thyme

8 fingerling potatoes, halved lengthwise

1 cup baby carrots

Black pepper

Chopped fresh Italian parsley (optional)

1. Combine flour and ½ teaspoon salt in large resealable food storage bag. Add beef; toss to coat. Press Sauté; heat 1 tablespoon oil in pot. Add half of beef; cook about 5 minutes or until browned. Remove to plate; repeat with remaining oil and beef.

2. Add broth, onion, mushrooms, garlic powder, remaining 1 teaspoon salt, basil, oregano, rosemary, marjoram, sage and thyme to pot; mix well. Return beef to pot. Secure lid and move pressure release valve to sealing or locked position. Cook at high pressure 30 minutes.

3. When cooking is complete, press Cancel and use quick release.

4. Add potatoes and carrots to pot. Secure lid and move pressure release valve to sealing or locked position. Cook at high pressure 10 minutes.

5. When cooking is complete, press Cancel and use quick release. Season with additional salt and pepper, if desired. Garnish with parsley.

MAKES 8 SERVINGS

TEX-MEX CHILI

4 slices bacon, chopped

⅓ cup all-purpose flour

1½ teaspoons salt, divided

¼ teaspoon black pepper

2 pounds boneless beef top round or chuck shoulder steak, cut into ½-inch pieces

1 medium onion, chopped, plus additional for garnish

2 cloves garlic, minced

1¼ cups water

¼ cup chili powder

1 teaspoon dried oregano

1 teaspoon ground cumin

½ to 1 teaspoon ground red pepper

½ teaspoon hot pepper sauce

1. Press Sauté; cook bacon in pot until crisp. Remove to paper towel-lined plate.

2. Combine flour, ½ teaspoon salt and black pepper in large resealable food storage bag. Add beef; toss to coat. Add beef to bacon drippings in two batches; cook about 5 minutes or until browned. Remove to plate.

3. Add onion to pot; cook and stir 3 minutes or until softened. Add garlic; cook and stir 1 minute. Return beef and bacon to pot. Add water, chili powder, remaining 1 teaspoon salt, oregano, cumin, red pepper and hot pepper sauce; cook and stir 2 minutes, scraping up browned bits from bottom of pot.

4. Secure lid and move pressure release valve to sealing or locked position. Cook at high pressure 20 minutes.

5. When cooking is complete, use natural release for 10 minutes, then release remaining pressure. Serve with additional onion, if desired.

MAKES 4 TO 6 SERVINGS

TIP: Texas chili doesn't contain any beans. But if you want to stretch this recipe and dilute some of the spiciness—and you don't live in Texas!—you can add canned pinto beans to the chili after the pressure has been released. Press Sauté and cook until the beans are heated through.

ITALIAN SHORT RIBS

2 tablespoons vegetable oil

3 pounds bone-in beef short ribs, trimmed and cut into 3-inch pieces

1 teaspoon Italian seasoning

¾ teaspoon salt

¼ teaspoon black pepper

1½ cups chopped leeks (2 to 3 leeks)

½ cup dry white wine

¾ cup pitted kalamata or oil-cured olives

1¼ cups prepared pasta sauce

Parmesan Polenta (recipe follows, optional)

1. Press Sauté; heat oil in pot. Add short ribs in batches; cook about 8 minutes or until browned on all sides. Remove to plate; season with Italian seasoning, salt and pepper. Drain off all but 1 tablespoon fat.

2. Add leeks to pot; cook and stir 2 minutes or until softened. Add wine; cook until almost evaporated, scraping up browned bits from bottom of pot. Return short ribs to pot with olives; pour pasta sauce over short ribs.

3. Secure lid and move pressure release valve to sealing or locked position. Cook at high pressure 30 minutes.

4. When cooking is complete, use natural release for 10 minutes, then release remaining pressure. Meanwhile, prepare Parmesan Polenta, if desired. Serve ribs and sauce with polenta.

MAKES 4 SERVINGS

PARMESAN POLENTA: Bring 2 cups water to a boil in large nonstick saucepan. Gradually whisk in 1 cup instant polenta until smooth and thick. Stir in ½ cup grated Parmesan cheese. Season with salt and pepper.

CHILI SPAGHETTI SUPPER

1 **pound lean ground beef**

1 **medium onion, chopped**

1 **teaspoon salt**

¼ **teaspoon black pepper**

1 **can (about 15 ounces) chili beans in mild sauce**

1 **can (about 14 ounces) diced tomatoes with Italian seasoning**

2 **teaspoons chili powder**

¼ **teaspoon garlic powder**

8 **ounces uncooked spaghetti**

½ **cup water**

1½ **cups (6 ounces) shredded sharp Cheddar cheese, divided**

¼ **cup sour cream**

1. Press Sauté; add beef, onion, salt and pepper to pot. Cook about 8 minutes or until beef is no longer pink, stirring to break up meat. Drain fat.

2. Stir in beans, tomatoes, chili powder and garlic powder; mix well. Break spaghetti in half; add to pot with water.

3. Secure lid and move pressure release valve to sealing or locked position. Cook at high pressure 5 minutes.

4. When cooking is complete, press Cancel and use quick release.

5. Press Sauté; stir in 1 cup cheese and sour cream. Cook and stir 1 minute or until cheese is melted and mixture is well blended. Turn off heat; let stand 3 minutes or until excess liquid is absorbed and pasta is tender. Sprinkle with remaining ½ cup cheese.

MAKES 4 TO 6 SERVINGS

DEVIL'S FIRE BEEF TACOS

1 boneless beef chuck roast (2½ pounds), cut into 4 pieces

1¼ teaspoons salt, divided

1¼ teaspoons *each* garlic powder, smoked paprika and ground cumin

1 large onion, divided

2 tablespoons olive oil, divided

⅔ cup beef broth, divided

1 red bell pepper, sliced

1 tomato, cut into wedges

2 cloves garlic, minced

1 to 2 canned chipotle peppers in adobo sauce

Juice of 1 lime

Corn or flour tortillas

Optional toppings: sliced bell peppers, avocado, diced onion, chopped fresh cilantro and/or lime wedges

1. Combine beef, 1 teaspoon salt, garlic powder, smoked paprika and cumin in medium bowl; toss to coat, pressing seasonings into beef. Cut onion in half; chop one half and cut second half into slices.

2. Press Sauté; heat 1 tablespoon oil in pot. Cook beef in two batches about 5 minutes or until browned. Remove to plate. Add chopped onion and 2 tablespoons broth; cook and stir 3 minutes or until onion is softened, scraping up browned bits from bottom of pot. Return beef to pot with remaining broth.

3. Secure lid and move pressure release valve to sealing or locked position. Cook at high pressure 60 minutes.

4. Meanwhile, preheat oven to 425°F. Combine bell pepper, tomato, sliced onion and garlic on large baking sheet. Drizzle with remaining 1 tablespoon oil; toss to coat. Roast 40 minutes or until vegetables are tender. Combine vegetables, chipotle pepper, lime juice and remaining ¼ teaspoon salt in food processor or blender; process until smooth.

5. When cooking is complete, use natural release for 10 minutes, then release remaining pressure. Remove beef to cutting board; let stand 10 minutes or until cool enough to handle.

6. Press Sauté; cook liquid in pot 10 minutes while beef is cooling. Shred beef with two forks. Combine shredded beef and ¾ cup cooking liquid in medium bowl; toss to coat. Discard remaining cooking liquid. Serve beef on tortillas with sauce and desired toppings.

MAKES 6 TO 8 SERVINGS

IRISH BEEF STEW

2½ tablespoons vegetable oil, divided

2 pounds boneless beef chuck roast, cut into 1-inch pieces

1½ teaspoons salt, divided

¾ teaspoon black pepper, divided

1 package (8 to 10 ounces) cremini mushrooms, quartered

1 medium onion, quartered

1 cup Guinness stout

1 tablespoon Dijon mustard

1 tablespoon tomato paste

1 tablespoon Worcestershire sauce

2 cloves garlic, minced

2 bay leaves

1 teaspoon dried thyme

1 teaspoon dried rosemary

1 pound small yellow potatoes (about 1¼ inches), halved

3 medium carrots, cut into ¾-inch pieces

3 medium parsnips, cut into ¾-inch pieces

2 teaspoons water

2 teaspoons cornstarch

1 cup frozen pearl onions

Chopped fresh parsley (optional)

1. Press Sauté; heat 2 tablespoons oil in pot. Season beef with 1 teaspoon salt and ½ teaspoon pepper. Cook beef in two batches about 5 minutes or until browned. Remove to plate.

2. Add remaining ½ tablespoon oil, mushrooms and onion quarters to pot; cook about 6 minutes or until mushrooms give off their liquid and begin to brown, stirring frequently. Add Guinness, mustard, tomato paste, Worcestershire sauce, garlic, bay leaves, thyme, rosemary, remaining ½ teaspoon salt and ¼ teaspoon pepper; cook and stir 3 minutes, scraping up browned bits from bottom of pot. Return beef and any accumulated juices to pot; mix well.

3. Secure lid and move pressure release valve to sealing or locked position. Cook at high pressure 30 minutes.

4. When cooking is complete, press Cancel and use quick release. Remove and discard bay leaves and large onion pieces. Add potatoes, carrots and parsnips to pot; mix well. Secure lid and move pressure release valve to sealing or locked position. Cook at high pressure 3 minutes. Meanwhile, stir water into cornstarch in small bowl until smooth.

5. When cooking is complete, press Cancel and use quick release. Press Sauté; stir pearl onions into stew. Add cornstarch mixture; cook 2 to 3 minutes or until stew thickens, stirring frequently. Garnish with parsley.

MAKES 6 SERVINGS

SWEET AND SAVORY BRISKET

1 teaspoon salt, divided

½ teaspoon black pepper

1 small beef brisket (2½ to 3 pounds), trimmed

1 large onion, thinly sliced

½ cup beef or chicken broth

⅓ cup chili sauce

1 tablespoon packed brown sugar

½ teaspoon dried thyme

¼ teaspoon ground cinnamon

2 large sweet potatoes, peeled and cut into 1-inch pieces

1 cup pitted prunes

¼ cup water

2 tablespoons cornstarch

1. Rub ½ teaspoon salt and pepper into all sides of beef. Place beef in pot; top with onion. Combine broth, chili sauce, brown sugar, thyme, cinnamon and remaining ½ teaspoon salt in small bowl; mix well. Pour over beef and onion.

2. Secure lid and move pressure release valve to sealing or locked position. Cook at high pressure 70 minutes.

3. When cooking is complete, use natural release for 10 minutes, then release remaining pressure. Remove beef to cutting board; tent with foil.

4. Add sweet potatoes and prunes to pot. Secure lid and move pressure release valve to sealing or locked position. Cook at high pressure 3 minutes. When cooking is complete, press Cancel and use quick release. Remove vegetables to bowl with slotted spoon.

5. Stir water into cornstarch in small bowl until smooth. Press Sauté; add cornstarch mixture to pot. Cook and stir 1 to 2 minutes or until sauce thickens.

6. Cut brisket into thin slices across the grain. Serve with sweet potato mixture and sauce.

MAKES 4 SERVINGS

PRESSURE COOKER MEAT LOAF

  1 **tablespoon olive oil**
  1 **small onion, finely chopped**
  ½ **red bell pepper, finely chopped**
  3 **cloves garlic, minced**
  1 **teaspoon dried oregano**
1½ **cups water**
  2 **pounds ground meat loaf mix or 1 pound *each* ground beef and ground pork**
  1 **egg**
  3 **tablespoons tomato paste**
  1 **teaspoon salt**
  ½ **teaspoon black pepper**

1. Press Sauté; heat oil in pot. Add onion, bell pepper, garlic and oregano; cook and stir 3 minutes or until vegetables are softened. Remove to large bowl; let cool 5 minutes. Wipe out pot with paper towels; add water and rack to pot.

2. Add meat loaf mix, egg, tomato paste, salt and black pepper to vegetable mixture; mix well. Tear off 18×12-inch piece of foil; fold in half crosswise to create 12×9-inch rectangle. Shape meat mixture into 7×5-inch oval on foil; bring up sides of foil to create pan, leaving top of meat loaf uncovered. Place foil with meat loaf on rack in pot.

3. Secure lid and move pressure release valve to sealing or locked position. Cook at high pressure 37 minutes.

4. When cooking is complete, press Cancel and use quick release. Remove meat loaf to cutting board; tent with foil. Let stand 10 minutes before slicing.

MAKES 6 SERVINGS

SHREDDED BEEF FAJITAS

- **1 beef flank steak (about 1 pound), cut into 2 pieces**
- **¼ teaspoon salt**
- **⅛ teaspoon black pepper**
- **1 tablespoon vegetable oil**
- **1 medium onion, chopped, divided**
- **1 medium green bell pepper, cut into ½-inch pieces, divided**
- **1 clove garlic, minced *or* ¼ teaspoon garlic powder**
- **1 can (about 10 ounces) diced tomatoes with mild green chiles**
- **½ package fajita seasoning mix (about 2 tablespoons)**
- **6 (8-inch) flour tortillas**
- **Optional toppings: sour cream, guacamole, shredded Cheddar cheese, salsa**

1. Season beef with salt and black pepper. Press Sauté; heat oil in pot. Add beef; cook 3 to 4 minutes per side or until browned. Remove to plate. Add half of onion and half of bell pepper to pot; cook and stir 2 minutes. Add garlic; cook and stir 30 seconds. Add tomatoes and fajita seasoning mix; cook 2 minutes, scraping up browned bits from bottom of pot. Return beef to pot, pressing into liquid.

2. Secure lid and move pressure release valve to sealing or locked position. Cook at high pressure 23 minutes.

3. When cooking is complete, use natural release for 10 minutes, then release remaining pressure. Remove beef to clean plate; let stand 10 minutes.

4. Meanwhile, press Sauté; add remaining half of onion and bell pepper to pot. Cook about 8 minutes or until bell pepper is crisp-tender and liquid is reduced, stirring occasionally.

5. Shred beef; return to pot and stir until blended. Serve beef mixture in tortillas with desired toppings.

MAKES 6 SERVINGS

BRAISED CHIPOTLE BEEF

1 **boneless beef chuck roast (about 3 pounds), cut into 1-inch pieces**

2 **teaspoons salt, divided**

¾ **teaspoon black pepper, divided**

3 **tablespoons vegetable oil, divided**

1 **large onion, cut into 1-inch pieces**

2 **red bell peppers, cut into 1½-inch pieces**

3 **tablespoons tomato paste**

1 **tablespoon minced garlic**

1 **tablespoon chipotle chili powder**

1 **tablespoon paprika**

1 **tablespoon ground cumin**

1 **teaspoon dried oregano**

¼ **cup water**

1 **can (about 14 ounces) diced tomatoes**

Hot cooked rice or tortillas (optional)

1. Pat beef dry with paper towels; season with ½ teaspoon salt and ¼ teaspoon black pepper.

2. Press Sauté; heat 2 tablespoons oil in pot. Add beef in two batches; cook about 5 minutes or until browned. Remove to plate.

3. Heat remaining 1 tablespoon oil in pot. Add onion; cook and stir 3 minutes or until softened. Add bell peppers; cook and stir 2 minutes. Add tomato paste, garlic, chili powder, paprika, cumin, oregano, remaining 1½ teaspoons salt and ½ teaspoon black pepper; cook and stir 1 minute. Stir in water, scraping up browned bits from bottom of pot. Return beef to pot with tomatoes; mix well.

4. Secure lid and move pressure release valve to sealing or locked position. Cook at high pressure 30 minutes.

5. When cooking is complete, use natural release for 10 minutes, then release remaining pressure. Serve with rice or tortillas, if desired.

MAKES 4 TO 6 SERVINGS

SERVING SUGGESTIONS: Add rice and/or beans to the Braised Chipotle Beef and use it as a filling for tacos or burritos. Or serve over mashed potatoes.

SHORTCUT BOLOGNESE

1 **tablespoon olive oil**

1 **pound ground beef**

1 **medium onion, chopped**

½ **small carrot, finely chopped**

½ **stalk celery, finely chopped**

3 **tablespoons tomato paste**

1 **cup dry white wine**

½ **cup milk**

⅛ **teaspoon ground nutmeg**

1 **can (about 14 ounces) whole tomatoes, undrained, coarsely chopped**

½ **cup beef broth**

1 **teaspoon salt**

1 **teaspoon dried basil**

½ **teaspoon dried thyme**

⅛ **teaspoon black pepper**

1 **bay leaf**

Hot cooked spaghetti

Grated Parmesan cheese (optional)

1. Press Sauté; heat oil in pot. Add beef; cook about 8 minutes or until all liquid evaporates, stirring to break up meat. Drain fat.

2. Add onion, carrot and celery to pot; cook and stir 4 minutes. Add tomato paste; cook and stir 2 minutes. Add wine; cook about 5 minutes or until wine has almost evaporated. Add milk and nutmeg; cook and stir 3 to 4 minutes or until milk has almost evaporated. Stir in tomatoes with liquid, broth, salt, basil, thyme, pepper and bay leaf; mix well.

3. Secure lid and move pressure release valve to sealing or locked position. Cook at high pressure 18 minutes.

4. When cooking is complete, press Cancel and use quick release. Remove and discard bay leaf. Serve sauce with spaghetti; top with cheese, if desired.

MAKES 4 SERVINGS

CORNED BEEF AND CABBAGE

- **1 corned beef brisket (3 to 4 pounds) with seasoning packet**
- **2 cups water**
- **1 head cabbage (1½ pounds), cut into 6 wedges**
- **1 package (16 ounces) baby carrots**

1. Place corned beef in pot, fat side up; sprinkle with seasoning. Pour water into pot.

2. Secure lid and move pressure release valve to sealing or locked position. Cook at high pressure 90 minutes.

3. When cooking is complete, use natural release for 10 minutes, then release remaining pressure. Remove beef to cutting board; tent with foil.

4. Add cabbage and carrots to pot. Secure lid and move pressure release valve to sealing or locked position. Cook at high pressure 4 minutes. When cooking is complete, press Cancel and use quick release.

5. Slice beef; serve with vegetables.

MAKES 3 TO 4 SERVINGS

MOLE CHILI

2 tablespoons olive oil, divided

1½ pounds boneless beef chuck, cut into 1-inch pieces

2 medium onions, chopped

5 cloves garlic, minced

1 cup beef broth, divided

1 can (about 14 ounces) fire-roasted diced tomatoes

2 corn tortillas, each cut into 4 wedges

2 tablespoons chili powder

1 tablespoon ancho chili powder

1 teaspoon dried oregano

1 teaspoon ground cumin

¾ teaspoon salt

¾ teaspoon ground cinnamon

½ teaspoon black pepper

1 can (about 15 ounces) red kidney beans, rinsed and drained

1½ ounces semisweet chocolate, chopped

1. Press Sauté; heat 1 tablespoon oil in pot. Add beef in two batches; cook about 5 minutes or until browned. Remove to plate.

2. Add remaining 1 tablespoon oil, onions and garlic to pot; cook and stir about 3 minutes or until onions are softened. Stir in ½ cup broth, scraping up browned bits from bottom of pot. Stir in remaining ½ cup broth, beef, tomatoes, tortillas, chili powders, oregano, cumin, salt, cinnamon and pepper; mix well.

3. Secure lid and move pressure release valve to sealing or locked position. Cook at high pressure 30 minutes.

4. When cooking is complete, use natural release for 15 minutes, then release remaining pressure.

5. Press Sauté; add beans and chocolate to pot. Cook and stir 2 minutes or until chocolate is melted and beans are heated through.

MAKES 4 SERVINGS

PORK & LAMB

PORK PICADILLO

1 tablespoon olive oil

1 pound boneless pork country-style ribs, trimmed and cut into ½-inch pieces

1 onion, chopped

2 cloves garlic, minced

1 can (about 14 ounces) diced tomatoes

½ cup raisins

2 tablespoons cider vinegar

2 canned chipotle peppers in adobo sauce, chopped

½ teaspoon salt

½ teaspoon ground cumin

½ teaspoon ground cinnamon

1. Press Sauté; heat oil in pot. Add pork; cook about 6 minutes or until browned, stirring occasionally. Add onion; cook and stir 2 minutes. Add garlic; cook and stir 30 seconds. Stir in tomatoes, raisins, vinegar, chipotle peppers, salt, cumin and cinnamon, scraping up browned bits from bottom of pot.

2. Secure lid and move pressure release valve to sealing or locked position. Cook at high pressure 25 minutes.

3. When cooking is complete, use natural release for 10 minutes, then release remaining pressure. Stir pork mixture with tongs, shredding pork into smaller pieces.

MAKES 4 SERVINGS

PORK ROAST WITH FRUIT

2 cups water

2 tablespoons salt

1 tablespoon sugar

1 teaspoon dried thyme

1 bay leaf

½ teaspoon black pepper

1 boneless pork loin roast
(3 to 3½ pounds)

1 tablespoon olive oil

⅓ cup dry red wine
Juice of ½ lemon

2 cloves garlic, minced

2 cups green grapes

1 cup dried apricots

1 cup dried prunes

1. Combine water, salt, sugar, thyme, bay leaf and pepper in large resealable food storage bag. Add pork; seal bag and turn to coat. Refrigerate overnight or up to 2 days, turning occasionally.

2. Remove pork from brine; discard liquid. Pat dry with paper towels. Press Sauté; heat oil in pot. Add pork; cook about 10 minutes or until browned on all sides. Remove to plate. Add wine, lemon juice and garlic; cook and stir 1 minute, scraping up browned bits from bottom of pot. Add grapes, apricots and prunes; mix well. Return pork to pot.

3. Secure lid and move pressure release valve to sealing or locked position. Cook at high pressure 20 minutes.

4. When cooking is complete, use natural release. Remove pork to cutting board; tent with foil and let stand 10 minutes before slicing.

5. Meanwhile, press Sauté; cook 10 minutes or until sauce is reduced and thickens slightly. Slice pork; serve with sauce.

MAKES 8 SERVINGS

GHORMEH SABZI (PERSIAN GREEN STEW)

1½ **pounds boneless leg of lamb, cut into 1-inch cubes**

1 **teaspoon ground turmeric**

¾ **teaspoon salt, divided**

½ **teaspoon curry powder**

½ **teaspoon ground black pepper, divided**

2 **tablespoons olive oil, divided**

2 **medium onions, chopped**

1 **package (5 ounces) baby spinach, chopped**

2 **cups chopped fresh Italian parsley**

6 **green onions, chopped**

1 **cup chopped fresh cilantro**

1 **can (about 15 ounces) cannellini beans, rinsed and drained**

½ **cup beef broth**

2 **tablespoons lime juice**

Hot cooked basmati rice

1. Combine lamb, turmeric, ½ teaspoon salt, curry powder and ¼ teaspoon pepper in large bowl; toss to coat. Press Sauté; heat 1 tablespoon oil in pot. Cook lamb in two batches about 4 minutes or until browned, stirring occasionally. Remove to plate.

2. Add remaining 1 tablespoon oil, onions and remaining ¼ teaspoon salt to pot; adjust heat to low. Cook 5 to 7 minutes or until onions begin to brown, stirring occasionally. Add spinach, parsley, green onions and cilantro; cook 3 minutes or until spinach is wilted, scraping up browned bits from bottom of pot. Stir in lamb, beans and broth; mix well.

3. Secure lid and move pressure release valve to sealing or locked position. Cook at high pressure 20 minutes.

4. When cooking is complete, use natural release for 10 minutes, then release remaining pressure.

5. Press Sauté; stir in lime juice and remaining ¼ teaspoon pepper. Cook about 3 minutes or until liquid is reduced slightly. Serve over rice.

MAKES 6 SERVINGS

ONE-POT PASTA WITH SAUSAGE

1 tablespoon olive oil

1 pound smoked sausage (about 4 links), cut into ¼-inch slices

1 onion, diced

1 tablespoon tomato paste

2 cloves garlic, minced

1½ teaspoons dried oregano

¼ teaspoon red pepper flakes

1 can (28 ounces) whole tomatoes, undrained, crushed with hands or coarsely chopped

2½ cups water

1½ teaspoons salt

1 package (16 ounces) uncooked cellentani pasta

1½ cups frozen peas

½ cup grated Parmesan cheese

⅓ cup shredded fresh basil leaves, plus additional for garnish

1. Press Sauté; heat oil in pot. Add sausage; cook about 7 minutes or until browned, stirring occasionally. Add onion; cook and stir 3 minutes or until softened. Add tomato paste, garlic, oregano and red pepper flakes; cook and stir 1 minute. Add tomatoes with liquid, water and salt; cook 2 minutes, scraping up browned bits from bottom of pot. Stir in pasta; mix well.

2. Secure lid and move pressure release valve to sealing or locked position. Cook at high pressure 5 minutes.

3. When cooking is complete, press Cancel and use quick release.

4. Press Sauté; add peas to pot. Cook and stir 2 minutes. Turn off heat; stir in cheese and ⅓ cup basil. Cover pot with lid (do not lock) and let stand 2 minutes. Garnish with additional basil.

MAKES 6 SERVINGS

VARIATION: You can substitute 1 pound uncooked Italian sausage (about 4 links) for the smoked sausage. Remove the casings, cut into ½-inch pieces and proceed with the recipe as directed.

MAPLE SPICE RUBBED RIBS

3 teaspoons chili powder, divided

1¼ teaspoons ground coriander

1¼ teaspoons garlic powder, divided

¾ teaspoon salt

½ teaspoon black pepper

3 to 3½ pounds pork baby back ribs, trimmed and cut into 4-rib sections

4 tablespoons maple syrup, divided

1 can (8 ounces) tomato sauce

¼ teaspoon ground cinnamon

¼ teaspoon ground ginger

1. Combine 1½ teaspoons chili powder, coriander, ¾ teaspoon garlic powder, salt and pepper in small bowl; mix well. Brush ribs with 2 tablespoons maple syrup; rub with spice mixture. Place ribs in pot.

2. Combine tomato sauce, remaining 2 tablespoons maple syrup, 1½ teaspoons chili powder, ½ teaspoon garlic powder, cinnamon and ginger in medium bowl; mix well. Pour over ribs in pot; stir to coat ribs with sauce.

3. Secure lid and move pressure release valve to sealing or locked position. Cook at high pressure 25 minutes.

4. When cooking is complete, use natural release for 10 minutes, then release remaining pressure. Remove ribs to plate; tent with foil.

5. Press Sauté; cook about 10 minutes or until sauce thickens. Brush ribs with sauce; serve remaining sauce on the side.

MAKES 4 SERVINGS

BALSAMIC PORK ROAST WITH POTATOES

1½ teaspoons salt, divided

1 teaspoon garlic powder

1 teaspoon dried thyme

½ teaspoon black pepper

⅛ teaspoon red pepper flakes

1 boneless pork loin roast (2 to 2½ pounds)

3 tablespoons olive oil, divided

1 small onion, finely chopped

½ cup chicken broth or water, divided

¼ cup balsamic vinegar

1 tablespoon Worcestershire sauce

1½ pounds Yukon gold potatoes, cut into 1½-inch pieces

Fresh parsley sprigs (optional)

1. Combine 1 teaspoon salt, garlic powder, thyme, black pepper and red pepper flakes in small bowl; mix well. Rub mixture over all sides of pork. Press Sauté; heat 2 tablespoons oil in pot. Add pork; cook 8 to 10 minutes or until browned on all sides. Remove to plate.

2. Add onion and ¼ cup broth to pot; cook and stir about 3 minutes or until onion is softened. Stir in remaining broth, vinegar and Worcestershire sauce; mix well. Return pork to pot, turning to coat.

3. Secure lid and move pressure release valve to sealing or locked position. Cook at high pressure 12 minutes. Meanwhile, preheat broiler. Line baking sheet with foil. Place potatoes in steamer basket that fits inside pot.

4. When cooking is complete, press Cancel and use quick release. Place steamer basket with potatoes inside pot (resting on top of pork). Secure lid and move pressure release valve to sealing or locked position. Cook at high pressure 4 minutes. When cooking is complete, use natural release for 5 minutes, then release remaining pressure.

5. Combine potatoes, remaining 1 tablespoon oil and ½ teaspoon salt in large bowl; toss to coat. Spread potatoes in single layer on prepared baking sheet. Broil about 5 minutes per side or until lightly browned.

6. Meanwhile, remove pork to cutting board; tent with foil. Let stand 10 minutes before slicing. Press Sauté; cook liquid in pot about 10 minutes or until reduced by one third. Slice pork; serve with potatoes and sauce. Garnish with parsley.

MAKES 4 TO 6 SERVINGS

Dr. Leonard N. Johnson
34696 Matthews Rd
Eugene, OR 97405-8617

TACOS WITH CARNITAS

2 tablespoons chili powder

1 tablespoon salt

1 tablespoon dried oregano

1 teaspoon ground cumin

1 medium onion, quartered

2 pounds pork leg, shoulder or roast, trimmed, cut into 4 pieces

2 bay leaves

1½ cups water

Corn tortillas, warmed

Optional toppings: shredded romaine lettuce, salsa, crumbled Cotija or feta cheese, canned diced green chiles

1 can (4 ounces) diced green chiles

1. Combine chili powder, salt, oregano and cumin in small bowl; mix well. Place onion in pot; place pork on top of onion. Sprinkle all over with spice mixture. Add bay leaves. Pour water into pot.

2. Secure lid and move pressure release valve to sealing or locked position. Cook at high pressure 75 minutes.

3. When cooking is complete, use natural release for 10 minutes, then release remaining pressure. Remove pork from liquid with tongs; place in 13×9-inch baking pan or on baking sheet lined with foil. Preheat broiler.

4. Remove onion and bay leaves from liquid. Press Sauté; cook liquid 10 minutes. Meanwhile, separate pork into large shreds with tongs; spread out in baking pan. Broil about 3 minutes or until browned.

5. Pull pork into smaller shreds with tongs or two forks. Place pork in medium bowl; add 1 cup cooking liquid and toss to coat. Add additional liquid, if desired. Serve pork in tortillas with desired toppings.

MAKES 6 SERVINGS

LAMB AND CHICKPEA STEW

1 cup dried chickpeas, soaked 8 hours or overnight

2 tablespoons vegetable oil, divided

1 pound lamb stew meat

1 large onion, chopped

1 tablespoon minced garlic

1½ teaspoons salt

1½ teaspoons ground cumin

1 teaspoon ground turmeric

1 teaspoon ground coriander

1 teaspoon ground cinnamon

¼ teaspoon black pepper

1 can (about 14 ounces) diced tomatoes

1½ cups chicken broth

½ cup chopped dried apricots, divided

¼ cup chopped fresh Italian parsley

2 tablespoons lemon juice

1 tablespoon honey

Hot cooked couscous

1. Drain and rinse chickpeas. Press Sauté; heat 1 tablespoon oil in pot. Add lamb; cook 6 minutes or until browned, stirring occasionally. Add remaining 1 tablespoon oil and onion to pot; cook and stir 3 minutes or until softened. Add garlic, salt, cumin, turmeric, coriander, cinnamon and pepper; cook and stir 1 minute. Add tomatoes and broth; cook and stir 2 minutes, scraping up browned bits from bottom of pot. Stir in chickpeas and ¼ cup apricots; mix well.

2. Secure lid and move pressure release valve to sealing or locked position. Cook at high pressure 20 minutes.

3. When cooking is complete, use natural release for 10 minutes, then release remaining pressure.

4. Press Sauté; add remaining ¼ cup apricots to pot. Cook 5 minutes or until sauce is reduced and thickens slightly, stirring frequently. Stir in parsley, lemon juice and honey. Serve over couscous.

MAKES 4 TO 6 SERVINGS

HOT AND SWEET SAUSAGE SANDWICHES

1½ cups pasta sauce

1 large sweet onion, cut into ¼-inch slices

1 medium green bell pepper, cut into ½-inch slices

1 medium red bell pepper, cut into ½-inch slices

1½ tablespoons packed dark brown sugar

1 package (16 ounces) hot Italian sausage links (5 sausages)

5 Italian rolls, split

1. Combine pasta sauce, onion, bell peppers and brown sugar in pot; mix well. Add sausages to pot; spoon some of sauce mixture over sausages.

2. Secure lid and move pressure release valve to sealing or locked position. Cook at high pressure 5 minutes.

3. When cooking is complete, use natural release for 10 minutes, then release remaining pressure. Remove sausages to plate; tent with foil.

4. Press Sauté; cook 10 minutes or until sauce is reduced by one third, stirring occasionally. Serve sausages in rolls; top with sauce.

MAKES 5 SERVINGS

TIP: If you have leftover sauce, refrigerate or freeze it and serve over pasta or polenta. Top with grated Parmesan cheese.

CIDER PORK AND ONIONS

1 tablespoon vegetable oil

1 bone-in pork shoulder roast
   (4 to 4½ pounds)*

4 onions, cut into ¼-inch slices
   (about 4 cups)

1 cup apple cider, divided

1 teaspoon salt, divided

4 cloves garlic, minced

1 teaspoon dried rosemary

½ teaspoon black pepper

*A 4-pound roast requires a pressure cooker
that is 8 quarts or larger to fit.

1. Press Sauté; heat oil in pot. Add pork; cook until browned on all sides. Remove to plate. Add onions, ¼ cup cider and ½ teaspoon salt to pot; cook 8 minutes or until onions are softened, scraping up browned bits from bottom of pot. Add garlic and rosemary, cook and stir 1 minute. Return pork to pot; sprinkle with remaining ½ teaspoon salt and pepper. Pour remaining ¾ cup cider over pork.

2. Secure lid and move pressure release valve to sealing or locked position. Cook at high pressure 75 minutes.

3. When cooking is complete, use natural release. Remove pork to platter; tent with foil.

4. Meanwhile, press Sauté; cook 10 to 15 minutes or until sauce is reduced by one third. Skim fat from sauce; season with additional salt and pepper. Cut pork; serve with sauce.

MAKES 8 SERVINGS

CHORIZO BURRITOS

15 ounces uncooked Mexican chorizo sausages, cut into bite-size pieces

2 green or red bell peppers, cut into 1-inch pieces

1 can (about 15 ounces) red beans, rinsed and drained

1 can (about 14 ounces) diced tomatoes

1 can (11 ounces) corn, drained

½ teaspoon ground cumin

½ teaspoon ground cinnamon

8 (8-inch) flour tortillas, warmed

2 cups hot cooked rice

Shredded Monterey Jack cheese

1. Combine chorizo, bell peppers, beans, tomatoes, corn, cumin and cinnamon in pot; mix well.

2. Secure lid and move pressure release valve to sealing or locked position. Cook at high pressure 10 minutes.

3. When cooking is complete, use natural release for 10 minutes, then release remaining pressure.

4. Press Sauté; cook about 5 minutes or until chorizo mixture thickens, stirring occasionally. Spoon mixture down centers of tortillas; top with rice and shredded cheese. Roll up tortillas; serve immediately.

MAKES 4 SERVINGS

SPICY-SWEET LAMB TAGINE

¾ **cup dried chickpeas, soaked 8 hours or overnight**

1 **tablespoon olive oil**

2 **pounds boneless lamb shoulder or leg, cut into 1½-inch pieces**

3 **medium onions, each cut into 8 wedges**

3 **cloves garlic, minced**

2 **teaspoons ground ginger**

2 **teaspoons ground cinnamon**

1 **teaspoon black pepper**

1½ **cups water**

1 **can (about 14 ounces) diced tomatoes**

2 **teaspoons salt**

1 **small butternut squash, peeled and cut into 1-inch pieces (about 3 cups)**

1 **cup chopped pitted prunes**

2 **medium zucchini, halved lengthwise and cut crosswise into ½-inch slices**

Saffron Couscous (recipe follows, optional)

¼ **cup chopped fresh cilantro or parsley**

1. Drain and rinse chickpeas. Press Sauté; heat oil in pot. Add lamb in two batches; cook about 5 minutes or until browned. Remove to plate.

2. Add onions, garlic, ginger, cinnamon and pepper to pot; cook and stir 30 seconds or until spices are fragrant. Add water; cook and stir 2 minutes, scraping up browned bits from bottom of pot. Stir in tomatoes, chickpeas and salt; mix well. Return lamb to pot.

3. Secure lid and move pressure release valve to sealing or locked position. Cook at high pressure 15 minutes. When cooking is complete, press Cancel and use quick release.

4. Add butternut squash and prunes to pot. Secure lid and move pressure release valve to sealing or locked position. Cook at high pressure 3 minutes. When cooking is complete, press Cancel and use quick release.

5. Press Sauté; add zucchini to pot. Cook 4 minutes or until zucchini is crisp-tender, stirring occasionally.

6. Meanwhile, prepare Saffron Couscous, if desired. Serve stew over couscous. Garnish with cilantro.

MAKES 4 TO 6 SERVINGS

SAFFRON COUSCOUS: Combine 2¼ cups water, 1 tablespoon butter, ¼ teaspoon salt and ¼ teaspoon crushed saffron threads in medium saucepan; bring to a boil over high heat. Stir in 1½ cups uncooked couscous. Remove from heat; cover and let stand 5 minutes or until liquid is absorbed. Fluff with fork.

PULLED PORK SANDWICHES

2 tablespoons kosher salt

2 tablespoons packed brown sugar

2 tablespoons paprika

1 teaspoon dry mustard

1 teaspoon black pepper

1 boneless pork shoulder roast (about 3 pounds), cut into 3-inch pieces

1 cup ketchup

⅓ cup cider vinegar

6 to 8 large rolls or hamburger buns, split

¾ cup barbecue sauce

1. Preheat oven to 325°F. Combine salt, brown sugar, paprika, mustard and pepper in small bowl; mix well. Rub mixture over all sides of pork.

2. Combine ketchup and vinegar in pot; mix well. Place pork pieces in sauce; do not stir.

3. Secure lid and move pressure release valve to sealing or locked position. Cook at high pressure 60 minutes.

4. When cooking is complete, use natural release for 10 minutes, then release remaining pressure. Remove pork to cutting board or large plate. Reserve ½ cup cooking liquid from pot.

5. Shred pork into bite-size pieces when cool enough to handle. Toss with reserved cooking liquid, if desired. Serve warm on rolls with barbecue sauce.

MAKES 6 TO 8 SERVINGS

CHILI SPICED PORK LOIN

1 **boneless pork loin roast (2 to 2½ pounds), trimmed**

1¼ **cups orange juice, divided**

1 **cup chopped onion**

2 **cloves garlic, minced**

1 **tablespoon cider vinegar**

1½ **teaspoons chili powder**

1 **teaspoon salt**

¼ **teaspoon dried thyme**

¼ **teaspoon ground cumin**

¼ **teaspoon ground cinnamon**

⅛ **teaspoon ground allspice**

⅛ **teaspoon ground cloves**

2 **tablespoons olive oil**

Fruit Chutney (recipe follows, optional)

1. Place pork in large resealable food storage bag or glass dish. Combine ½ cup orange juice, onion, garlic, vinegar, chili powder, salt, thyme, cumin, cinnamon, allspice and cloves in small bowl; mix well. Pour marinade over pork; seal bag and turn to coat. Refrigerate 2 to 4 hours or overnight.

2. Remove pork from marinade; reserve marinade. Press Sauté; heat oil in pot. Add pork; cook about 6 minutes or until browned on all sides. Stir in remaining ¾ cup orange juice and reserved marinade, scraping up browned bits from bottom of pot.

3. Secure lid and move pressure release valve to sealing or locked position. Cook at high pressure 20 minutes.

4. When cooking is complete, use natural release for 10 minutes, then release remaining pressure. Remove pork to cutting board; tent with foil. Let stand 10 minutes before slicing.

5. Meanwhile, prepare Fruit Chutney, if desired. Or press Sauté; cook until liquid in pot is reduced by one third. Serve with pork.

MAKES 4 SERVINGS

FRUIT CHUTNEY: Add ¼ cup apricot preserves or orange marmalade to cooking liquid after removing pork from pot. Press Sauté; cook 10 minutes, stirring occasionally. Add 1 diced mango, ½ cup diced fresh pineapple, 2 minced green onions and 1 tablespoon minced jalapeño pepper; cook and stir 5 minutes. Serve with pork.

SPICY SAUSAGE AND PENNE PASTA

1 pound bulk hot Italian sausage

1 cup chopped onion

2 cloves garlic, minced

2 teaspoons salt

1 teaspoon dried oregano

1 teaspoon dried basil

2 cans (about 14 ounces each) diced tomatoes

1½ cups water

8 ounces uncooked penne pasta

3 cups broccoli florets (from 1 medium head)

½ cup shredded Asiago or Romano cheese

1. Press Sauté; crumble sausage into pot. Add onion; cook 10 minutes or until sausage is cooked through, stirring frequently. Add garlic, salt, oregano and basil; cook and stir 1 minute. Stir in tomatoes, water and pasta; mix well.

2. Secure lid and move pressure release valve to sealing or locked position. Cook at high pressure 3 minutes.

3. When cooking is complete, press Cancel and use quick release. Stir in broccoli. Secure lid and move pressure release valve to sealing or locked position. Cook at high pressure 0 minutes. (Set cooking time for 0 minutes; pressure cooker will beep as soon as contents reach pressure.)

4. When cooking is complete, press Cancel and use quick release. Stir pasta; sprinkle with cheese.

MAKES 4 TO 6 SERVINGS

JERK PORK AND SWEET POTATO STEW

2 tablespoons all-purpose flour

1 teaspoon salt

¼ teaspoon black pepper

1¼ pounds boneless pork shoulder, cut into 1-inch pieces

2 tablespoons vegetable oil

4 tablespoons minced green onions, divided

1 small jalapeño pepper,* seeded and minced

1 clove garlic, minced

⅛ teaspoon ground allspice

1 cup chicken broth

1 large sweet potato, peeled and cut into ¾-inch pieces

1 cup thawed frozen corn

1 tablespoon lime juice

Hot cooked rice (optional)

Jalapeño peppers can sting and irritate the skin, so wear rubber gloves when handling and do not touch your eyes.

1. Combine flour, salt and black pepper in large resealable food storage bag. Add pork; toss to coat. Press Sauté; heat oil in pot. Add pork in two batches, cook about 5 minutes or until browned. Remove to plate.

2. Add 2 tablespoons green onions, jalapeño, garlic and allspice to pot; cook and stir 30 seconds. Stir in broth, scraping up browned bits from bottom of pot. Return pork to pot.

3. Secure lid and move pressure release valve to sealing or locked position. Cook at high pressure 18 minutes.

4. When cooking is complete, press Cancel and use quick release. Add sweet potato to pot. Secure lid and move pressure release valve to sealing or locked position. Cook at high pressure 2 minutes.

5. When cooking is complete, press Cancel and use quick release.

6. Stir in corn, remaining 2 tablespoons green onions and lime juice; let stand 2 minutes or until corn is heated through. Serve with rice, if desired.

MAKES 4 SERVINGS

SEAFOOD

SEA BASS WITH VEGETABLES

2 tablespoons butter or olive oil

2 bulbs fennel, thinly sliced

3 large carrots, julienned

3 large leeks, thinly sliced

¾ teaspoon salt, divided

¼ teaspoon plus ⅛ teaspoon black pepper, divided

6 sea bass fillets or other firm-fleshed white fish (6 to 8 ounces each)

¼ cup water

1. Press Sauté; melt butter in pot. Add fennel, carrots and leeks; cook about 8 minutes or until vegetables are softened and beginning to brown, stirring occasionally. Stir in ½ teaspoon salt and ¼ teaspoon pepper. Remove half of vegetables to plate.

2. Season sea bass with remaining ¼ teaspoon salt and ⅛ teaspoon pepper; place on top of vegetables in pot. Top with remaining vegetables. Drizzle with water.

3. Secure lid and move pressure release valve to sealing or locked position. Cook at low pressure 4 minutes.

4. When cooking is complete, press Cancel and use quick release. Serve sea bass with vegetables.

MAKES 6 SERVINGS

SAVORY COD STEW

8 ounces bacon, chopped

1 large onion, diced

1 large carrot, diced

2 stalks celery, diced

2 cloves garlic, minced

1 can (28 ounces) plum tomatoes, undrained, coarsely chopped

2 potatoes, peeled and diced

1 cup clam juice

3 tablespoons tomato paste

3 tablespoons chopped fresh Italian parsley

½ teaspoon salt

¼ teaspoon black pepper

3 saffron threads

2½ pounds fresh cod, skin removed, cut into 1½-inch pieces

1. Press Sauté; cook bacon in pot until crisp. Drain off all but 2 tablespoons drippings.

2. Add onion, carrot, celery and garlic to pot; cook and stir 5 minutes or until vegetables are softened. Add tomatoes with liquid, potatoes, clam juice, tomato paste, parsley, salt, pepper and saffron; cook and stir 2 minutes.

3. Secure lid and move pressure release valve to sealing or locked position. Cook at high pressure 2 minutes.

4. When cooking is complete, press Cancel and use quick release.

5. Add cod to pot. Secure lid and move pressure release valve to sealing or locked position. Cook at low pressure 1 minute.

6. When cooking is complete, press Cancel and use quick release.

MAKES 6 TO 8 SERVINGS

ORZO RISOTTO WITH SHRIMP AND VEGETABLES

1 tablespoon olive oil

1 medium zucchini, halved and sliced

2 teaspoons grated lemon peel

2 cans (about 14 ounces each) chicken broth

1¼ cups uncooked orzo pasta

1 cup sliced mushrooms

½ cup chopped onion

2 cloves garlic, minced

¾ teaspoon salt

¾ teaspoon dried sage

¼ teaspoon dried thyme

8 ounces medium raw shrimp, peeled and deveined (with tails on)

¾ cup frozen peas, thawed

¼ cup grated Parmesan cheese

Black pepper

1. Press Sauté; heat oil in pot. Add zucchini and lemon peel; cook and stir 2 to 3 minutes or until zucchini is tender. Remove to small bowl.

2. Add broth, orzo, mushrooms, onion, garlic, salt, sage and thyme to pot; mix well. Secure lid and move pressure release valve to sealing or locked position. Cook at high pressure 4 minutes.

3. When cooking is complete, press Cancel and use quick release.

4. Press Sauté; adjust heat to low. Add shrimp and peas to pot; cook about 3 minutes or until shrimp are pink and opaque, stirring frequently. Stir in cheese; season with pepper.

MAKES 4 SERVINGS

MISO SALMON

½ cup water

2 green onions, cut into 2-inch pieces

¼ cup yellow miso paste

¼ cup soy sauce

2 tablespoons sake

2 tablespoons mirin

1½ teaspoons grated fresh ginger

1 teaspoon minced garlic

6 salmon fillets (about 4 ounces each)

Hot cooked rice (optional)

Thinly sliced green onions (optional)

1. Combine water, 2 green onions, miso paste, soy sauce, sake, mirin, ginger and garlic in pot; mix well. Add salmon to pot, skin side down.

2. Secure lid and move pressure release valve to sealing or locked position. Cook at low pressure 4 minutes.

3. When cooking is complete, press Cancel and use quick release. Serve salmon with rice, if desired. Garnish with sliced green onions; drizzle with cooking liquid.

MAKES 6 SERVINGS

NEW ENGLAND FISH CHOWDER

4 slices bacon, chopped

1 cup chopped onion

½ cup chopped celery

2 cups plus 2 tablespoons water, divided

2 cups peeled russet potatoes, cut into 1-inch pieces

1 teaspoon dried dill weed

½ teaspoon dried thyme

½ teaspoon salt

½ teaspoon black pepper

1 bay leaf

1 pound cod, haddock or halibut fillets, skinned, boned, and cut into 1-inch pieces*

2 tablespoons all-purpose flour

2 cups milk or half-and-half

*If fillets are very thin, cut into larger pieces to prevent overcooking.

1. Press Sauté; cook bacon in pot until crisp. Remove to paper towel-lined plate.

2. Add onion and celery to pot; cook and stir 3 minutes or until vegetables are softened. Stir in 2 cups water, potatoes, dill weed, thyme, salt, pepper and bay leaf; mix well.

3. Secure lid and move pressure release valve to sealing or locked position. Cook at high pressure 2 minutes. When cooking is complete, press Cancel and use quick release.

4. Add cod to pot. Secure lid and move pressure release valve to sealing or locked position. Cook at low pressure 1 minute. When cooking is complete, press Cancel and use quick release.

5. Stir remaining 2 tablespoons water into flour in small bowl until smooth. Press Sauté; adjust heat to low. Add flour mixture to pot; cook and stir 3 minutes or until soup thickens. Add milk and bacon; cook 2 minutes or until heated through, stirring gently. (Do not boil.) Remove and discard bay leaf.

MAKES 4 TO 6 SERVINGS

SHRIMP JAMBALAYA

2 cans (about 14 ounces each) diced tomatoes, drained

1 medium onion, chopped

1 medium red bell pepper, chopped

1 stalk celery, chopped

2 tablespoons minced garlic

2 teaspoons dried parsley flakes

2 teaspoons dried oregano

1 teaspoon salt

1 teaspoon hot pepper sauce

½ teaspoon dried thyme

2 pounds medium raw shrimp, peeled and deveined (with tails on)

Hot cooked rice

1. Combine tomatoes, onion, bell pepper, celery, garlic, parsley flakes, oregano, salt, hot pepper sauce and thyme in pot; mix well.

2. Secure lid and move pressure release valve to sealing or locked position. Cook at high pressure 9 minutes.

3. When cooking is complete, press Cancel and use quick release.

4. Press Sauté; add shrimp to pot. Cook 5 minutes or until shrimp are pink and opaque and liquid is slightly reduced. Serve over rice.

MAKES 6 SERVINGS

SCALLOPS WITH HERB TOMATO SAUCE

2 tablespoons vegetable oil

1 medium red onion, chopped

1 clove garlic, minced

3½ cups fresh tomatoes, peeled*

1 can (6 ounces) tomato paste

¼ cup dry red wine

2 tablespoons chopped fresh Italian parsley

1 tablespoon chopped fresh oregano

1 teaspoon salt

¼ teaspoon black pepper

1½ pounds fresh scallops, cleaned and drained

Hot cooked pasta or rice (optional)

*To peel tomatoes, score "x" in bottom of tomatoes and place one at a time in simmering water about 10 seconds. (Add 30 seconds if tomatoes are not fully ripened.) Immediately plunge into bowl of cold water for another 10 seconds. Peel skin with a knife.

1. Press Sauté; heat oil in pot. Add onion and garlic; cook and stir 3 to 4 minutes or until onion is translucent. Stir in tomatoes, tomato paste, wine, parsley, oregano, salt and pepper; mix well.

2. Secure lid and move pressure release valve to sealing or locked position. Cook at high pressure 8 minutes.

3. When cooking is complete, press Cancel and use quick release. Taste sauce; season with additional salt and pepper if necessary.

4. Press Sauté; add scallops to pot. Cook 1 minute or until sauce begins to simmer. Press Cancel; cover pot with lid and let stand 8 minutes or until scallops are opaque. Serve with pasta, if desired.

MAKES 4 SERVINGS

ITALIAN FISH SOUP

1 can (about 14 ounces) Italian-seasoned diced tomatoes

1 cup chicken broth

1 small bulb fennel, chopped (about 1 cup), fronds reserved for garnish

3 cloves garlic, minced

1 tablespoon olive oil

½ teaspoon saffron threads, crushed (optional)

½ teaspoon dried basil

¼ teaspoon salt

¼ teaspoon red pepper flakes

8 ounces skinless halibut or cod fillets, cut into 1-inch pieces

8 ounces medium raw shrimp, peeled and deveined (with tails on)

1. Combine tomatoes, broth, chopped fennel, garlic, oil, saffron, if desired, basil, salt and red pepper flakes in pot; mix well.

2. Secure lid and move pressure release valve to sealing or locked position. Cook at high pressure 3 minutes. When cooking is complete, press Cancel and use quick release.

3. Add halibut to pot. Secure lid and move pressure release valve to sealing or locked position. Cook at low pressure 1 minute.

4. When cooking is complete, press Cancel and use quick release.

5. Press Sauté; add shrimp to pot. Cook 2 to 3 minutes or until shrimp are pink and opaque, stirring occasionally. Garnish with fennel fronds.

MAKES 4 SERVINGS

GREEK-STYLE SALMON

1 tablespoon olive oil

1 can (about 14 ounces) diced tomatoes, drained

¼ cup pitted black olives, coarsely chopped

¼ cup pitted green olives, coarsely chopped

3 tablespoons lemon juice

2 tablespoons chopped fresh Italian parsley

1 tablespoon capers, rinsed and drained

2 cloves garlic, thinly sliced

¼ teaspoon black pepper

1 pound salmon fillets

1. Press Sauté; heat oil in pot. Add tomatoes, olives, lemon juice, parsley, capers, garlic and pepper; bring to a simmer, stirring frequently.

2. Secure lid and move pressure release valve to sealing or locked position. Cook at high pressure 4 minutes.

3. When cooking is complete, press Cancel and use quick release.

4. Place salmon in pot, skin side down. Press Sauté; bring to a simmer. Turn off heat; cover pot with lid and let stand 10 minutes or until fish begins to flake when tested with fork.

MAKES 4 SERVINGS

CREAMY CRAB CHOWDER

1 tablespoon butter

1 cup finely chopped onion

2 cloves garlic, minced

1 cup chopped celery

½ cup chopped green bell pepper

½ cup chopped red bell pepper

3 cans (about 14 ounces each) chicken broth

3 cups diced peeled russet potatoes

1 teaspoon salt

½ teaspoon dried thyme

½ teaspoon black pepper

⅛ teaspoon ground red pepper

2 cans (6½ ounces each) lump crabmeat, drained and flaked

1 package (10 ounces) frozen corn

½ cup half-and-half

1. Press Sauté; melt butter in pot. Add onion and garlic; cook and stir 3 minutes or until onion is softened. Add celery and bell peppers; cook and stir 4 minutes or until vegetables begin to soften. Stir in broth, potatoes, salt, thyme, black pepper and ground red pepper; mix well.

2. Secure lid and move pressure release valve to sealing or locked position. Cook at high pressure 6 minutes.

3. When cooking is complete, press Cancel and use quick release.

4. Press Sauté; add crabmeat, corn and half-and-half to pot. Cook and stir 2 minutes or until soup begins to simmer.

MAKES 6 TO 8 SERVINGS

VEGETABLES

CIDER VINAIGRETTE-GLAZED BEETS

6 medium red and/or golden beets (about 3 pounds)

1 cup water

2 tablespoons cider vinegar

1 tablespoon extra virgin olive oil

1 teaspoon Dijon mustard

½ teaspoon packed brown sugar

¾ teaspoon salt

¼ teaspoon black pepper

⅓ cup crumbled blue cheese (optional)

1. Cut tops off beets, leaving at least 1 inch of stems. Scrub beets under cold running water with soft vegetable brush, being careful not to break skins. Pour 1 cup water into pot. Place rack in pot; place beets on rack (or use steamer basket to hold beets).

2. Secure lid and move pressure release valve to sealing or locked position. Cook at high pressure 22 minutes.

3. When cooking is complete, use natural release for 10 minutes, then release remaining pressure. Check doneness by inserting paring knife into beets; knife should go in easily. If not, cook an additional 2 to 4 minutes.

4. Whisk vinegar, oil, mustard, brown sugar, salt and pepper in medium bowl until well blended.

5. When beets are cool enough to handle, peel off skins and trim root ends. Cut into wedges. Add warm beets to vinaigrette; toss gently to coat. Sprinkle with cheese, if desired. Serve warm or at room temperature.

MAKES 6 SERVINGS

WARM POTATO SALAD

2 pounds fingerling potatoes

¾ cup water

3 slices thick-cut bacon, cut into ½-inch pieces

1 small onion, diced

2 tablespoons olive oil

¼ cup cider vinegar

2 tablespoons capers, drained

1 tablespoon Dijon mustard

¾ teaspoon salt

¼ teaspoon black pepper

⅓ cup chopped fresh parsley

1. Combine potatoes and water in pot. Secure lid and move pressure release valve to sealing or locked position. Cook at high pressure 4 minutes.

2. When cooking is complete, press Cancel and use quick release. Drain potatoes; let stand until cool enough to handle. Dry out pot with paper towels.

3. Press Sauté; cook bacon in pot until crisp. Drain on paper towel-lined plate. Drain off all but 1 tablespoon drippings from pot. Adjust heat to low. Add onion and oil to pot; cook about 10 minutes or until onion begins to turn golden, stirring occasionally. Meanwhile, cut potatoes crosswise into ½-inch slices.

4. Add vinegar, capers, mustard, salt and pepper to pot; mix well. Turn off heat; stir in potatoes. Add parsley and bacon; stir gently to coat.

MAKES 6 TO 8 SERVINGS

PENNE WITH CHUNKY TOMATO SAUCE AND SPINACH

1 tablespoon olive oil

1 cup chopped onion

2 cloves garlic, minced

2 teaspoons salt

½ teaspoon dried oregano

½ teaspoon dried basil

¼ teaspoon red pepper flakes

¼ teaspoon black pepper

1 can (6 ounces) tomato paste

2 cups water

8 ounces uncooked penne pasta

1 package (5 ounces) baby spinach

1 large ripe tomato, seeded and chopped

¼ cup grated Parmesan cheese

¼ cup chopped fresh basil

1. Press Sauté; heat oil in pot. Add onion and garlic; cook and stir 3 minutes or until onion is softened. Add salt, oregano, dried basil, red pepper flakes and black pepper; cook and stir 30 seconds. Add tomato paste; cook and stir 1 minute. Add water; stir until well blended. Stir in pasta; mix well.

2. Secure lid and move pressure release valve to sealing or locked position. Cook at high pressure 4 minutes.

3. When cooking is complete, press Cancel and use quick release. Stir in spinach and tomato; cover and let stand 2 to 3 minutes or until spinach is wilted. Top with cheese and basil.

MAKES 4 SERVINGS

MASHED SWEET POTATOES AND PARSNIPS

2 large sweet potatoes (about 1½ pounds), peeled and cut into 1-inch pieces

2 medium parsnips (about 12 ounces), peeled and cut into ½-inch pieces

½ cup water

1 teaspoon salt

¼ cup evaporated milk

2 tablespoons butter

⅛ teaspoon ground nutmeg

¼ cup chopped fresh chives or green onions

1. Combine sweet potatoes, parsnips, water and salt in pot. Secure lid and move pressure release valve to sealing or locked position. Cook at high pressure 10 minutes.

2. When cooking is complete, press Cancel and use quick release.

3. Add milk, butter and nutmeg to pot; mash with potato masher until smooth. Stir in chives.

MAKES 6 SERVINGS

BUTTERNUT SQUASH WITH APPLES, CRANBERRIES AND WALNUTS

1 tablespoon butter

1 medium Granny Smith apple, peeled and cut into ½-inch pieces

3 cups cubed (about ¾ inch) peeled butternut squash

½ cup water

3 tablespoons dried cranberries

2 teaspoons packed brown sugar

½ teaspoon salt

¼ teaspoon ground cinnamon

⅛ teaspoon black pepper

2 tablespoons chopped walnuts

1. Press Sauté; melt butter in pot. Add apple; cook about 5 minutes or until tender, stirring occasionally. Remove to plate; set aside. Add squash, water, cranberries, brown sugar, salt, cinnamon and pepper to pot; stir until brown sugar is dissolved.

2. Secure lid and move pressure release valve to sealing or locked position. Cook at high pressure 1 minute.

3. When cooking is complete, press Cancel and use quick release.

4. Press Sauté; add cooked apples to pot. Cook 2 minutes or until heated through, stirring occasionally. Gently stir in walnuts.

MAKES 4 SERVINGS

THAI RED CURRY WITH TOFU

2 tablespoons vegetable oil

5 medium shallots, thinly sliced (about 1½ cups)

3 tablespoons Thai red curry paste

1 teaspoon minced garlic

1 teaspoon grated fresh ginger

1 can (about 13 ounces) unsweetened coconut milk

1 medium sweet potato, peeled and cut into 1-inch pieces

1 small eggplant, halved lengthwise then cut crosswise into ½-inch slices

1½ tablespoons soy sauce

1 tablespoon packed brown sugar

1 package (14 to 16 ounces) extra firm tofu, cut into 1-inch pieces

1 red bell pepper, cut into ¼-inch strips

½ cup green beans (1-inch pieces)

¼ cup chopped fresh basil

2 tablespoons lime juice

Hot cooked rice (optional)

1. Press Sauté; heat oil in pot. Add shallots; cook and stir 2 minutes or until softened. Add curry paste, garlic and ginger; cook and stir 1 minute. Stir in coconut milk, sweet potato, eggplant, soy sauce and brown sugar; mix well.

2. Secure lid and move pressure release valve to sealing or locked position. Cook at high pressure 4 minutes.

3. When cooking is complete, press Cancel and use quick release.

4. Add tofu, bell pepper and green beans to pot. Secure lid and move pressure release valve to sealing or locked position. Cook at low pressure 1 minute.

5. When cooking is complete, press Cancel and use quick release. Stir in basil and lime juice. Serve with rice, if desired.

MAKES 4 SERVINGS

VEGETARIAN CHILI

2 tablespoons olive oil

1 onion, finely chopped

2 medium carrots, chopped

1 red bell pepper, chopped

3 tablespoons chili powder

2 tablespoons tomato paste

2 tablespoons packed dark
   brown sugar

2 tablespoons ground cumin

3 cloves garlic, minced

1 tablespoon dried oregano

2 teaspoons salt

1 can (28 ounces) diced tomatoes

1 can (15 ounces) tomato sauce

1 can (about 15 ounces) small white
   beans, rinsed and drained

1 can (about 15 ounces) light kidney
   beans, rinsed and drained

1 can (about 15 ounces) dark kidney
   beans, rinsed and drained

1 can (about 15 ounces) pinto beans,
   rinsed and drained

1 can (4 ounces) diced green chiles

1 ounce unsweetened chocolate,
   chopped

1 tablespoon cider vinegar

1. Press Sauté; heat oil in pot. Add onion, carrots and bell pepper; cook and stir 5 minutes or until vegetables are softened. Add chili powder, tomato paste, brown sugar, cumin, garlic, oregano and salt; cook and stir 1 minute. Stir in tomatoes, tomato sauce, beans and chiles; mix well.

2. Secure lid and move pressure release valve to sealing or locked position. Cook at high pressure 10 minutes.

3. When cooking is complete, use natural release for 10 minutes, then release remaining pressure. Stir in chocolate and vinegar until blended.

MAKES 8 TO 10 SERVINGS

CAULIFLOWER AND POTATO MASALA

1 tablespoon olive or vegetable oil

2 teaspoons minced garlic

1 teaspoon minced fresh ginger

1 teaspoon salt

1 teaspoon cumin seeds *or*
  ½ teaspoon ground cumin

1 teaspoon ground coriander

1 teaspoon garam masala

1 can (about 14 ounces) diced
  tomatoes

1 head cauliflower (about
  1¼ pounds), broken into florets

1 pound red potatoes (2 large),
  peeled and cut into ½-inch wedges

2 tablespoons chopped fresh cilantro

1. Press Sauté; heat oil in pot. Add garlic, ginger, salt, cumin, coriander and garam masala; cook and stir about 30 seconds or until fragrant. Add tomatoes; cook and stir 1 minute. Add cauliflower and potatoes; mix well.

2. Secure lid and move pressure release valve to sealing or locked position. Cook at high pressure 2 minutes.

3. When cooking is complete, press Cancel and use quick release. Sprinkle with cilantro.

MAKES 6 SERVINGS

SHAKSHUKA

2 tablespoons extra virgin olive oil
1 large red bell pepper, chopped
1 medium onion, chopped
3 cloves garlic, minced
2 teaspoons sugar
2 teaspoons ground cumin
1 teaspoon paprika
1 teaspoon chili powder
½ teaspoon salt
¼ teaspoon red pepper flakes
1 can (28 ounces) crushed tomatoes
¾ cup crumbled feta cheese
4 eggs

1. Press Sauté; heat oil in pot. Add bell pepper and onion; cook and stir 3 minutes or until vegetables are softened. Add garlic, sugar, cumin, paprika, chili powder, salt and red pepper flakes; cook and stir 1 minute. Stir in tomatoes; mix well.

2. Secure lid and move pressure release valve to sealing or locked position. Cook at high pressure 10 minutes.

3. When cooking is complete, press Cancel and use quick release.

4. Stir in cheese. Make four wells in sauce for eggs, leaving space between each. Slide eggs, one at a time, into wells in sauce. (For best results, crack each egg into small bowl before sliding into sauce.)

5. Secure lid and move pressure release valve to sealing or locked position. Cook at low pressure 1 minute. When cooking is complete, press Cancel and use quick release. To cook eggs longer, press Sauté and cook until desired doneness.

MAKES 4 SERVINGS

COLCANNON

4 slices bacon, chopped

3 pounds russet potatoes, peeled and cut into 1-inch pieces

2 medium leeks, halved lengthwise and thinly sliced

½ cup water

1¼ teaspoons salt

¼ teaspoon black pepper

1 cup milk, divided

2 tablespoons butter, cut into pieces

½ small head savoy cabbage (about 1 pound), cored and thinly sliced (about 4 cups)

1. Press Sauté; cook bacon in pot until crisp. Remove to paper towel-lined plate. Add potatoes, leeks, water, salt and pepper to pot; mix well.

2. Secure lid and move pressure release valve to sealing or locked position. Cook at high pressure 5 minutes.

3. When cooking is complete, press Cancel and use quick release.

4. Press Sauté; add ½ cup milk and butter to pot. Cook and stir 1 minute, mashing potatoes until still slightly chunky. Add remaining ½ cup milk and cabbage; cook and stir 2 to 3 minutes or until cabbage is wilted. Stir in bacon.

MAKES 6 TO 8 SERVINGS

SUMMER SQUASH LASAGNA

2 tablespoons olive oil

1 onion, chopped

1 medium zucchini, cut crosswise into ¼-inch slices

1 medium yellow squash, cut crosswise into ¼-inch slices

2 cloves garlic, minced

1 teaspoon salt, divided

1 cup ricotta cheese

1½ cups (6 ounces) shredded mozzarella cheese, divided

½ cup grated Parmesan cheese, divided

¼ cup plus 2 tablespoons chopped fresh basil, divided

1 egg

¼ teaspoon black pepper

2¼ cups marinara sauce

8 oven-ready (no-boil) lasagna noodles

1 cup water

1. Spray 7-inch springform pan with nonstick cooking spray; set aside. Heat oil in large skillet over medium-high heat. Add onion, zucchini and yellow squash; cook and stir about 5 minutes or until vegetables are softened and lightly browned. Add garlic and ½ teaspoon salt; cook and stir 30 seconds.

2. Combine ricotta, ¼ cup mozzarella, ¼ cup Parmesan, ¼ cup basil, egg, remaining ½ teaspoon salt and pepper in medium bowl; mix well.

3. Spread ¼ cup marinara sauce in bottom of prepared springform pan. Layer with 2 noodles, breaking to fit. Spread one third of ricotta mixture over noodles. Top with one third of vegetables, ¼ cup mozzarella and ½ cup sauce. Repeat layers twice. For final layer, top with remaining 2 noodles, ½ cup sauce, ½ cup mozzarella and ¼ cup Parmesan. Cover pan tightly with foil.

4. Pour water into pot. Place pan on rack; lower rack into pot. Secure lid and move pressure release valve to sealing or locked position. Cook at high pressure 20 minutes.

5. When cooking is complete, use natural release. Carefully remove pan from pot. Remove foil.

6. If desired, preheat broiler and broil lasagna for 1 minute or until cheese is browned. Cool in pan 10 minutes. Remove side of pan; cut into squares or wedges. Sprinkle with remaining 2 tablespoons basil.

MAKES 4 TO 6 SERVINGS

CARIBBEAN SWEET POTATOES

2½ **pounds sweet potatoes, peeled and cut into 1-inch pieces**

8 **ounces shredded peeled carrots**

¾ **cup flaked coconut, divided**

½ **cup water**

¼ **cup (½ stick) butter, cut into pieces**

2 **tablespoons sugar**

1 **teaspoon salt**

½ **cup chopped walnuts, toasted***

2 **tablespoons lime juice**

1 **teaspoon grated lime peel**

*To toast walnuts, cook in small skillet over medium heat 6 to 8 minutes or until fragrant, stirring frequently.

1. Combine sweet potatoes, carrots, ½ cup coconut, water, butter, sugar and salt in pot; mix well.

2. Secure lid and move pressure release valve to sealing or locked position. Cook at high pressure 5 minutes.

3. Meanwhile, place remaining ¼ cup coconut in small skillet; cook 4 minutes or until lightly browned, stirring frequently.

4. When cooking is complete, press Cancel and use quick release.

5. Mash sweet potatoes in pot until desired consistency. Stir in walnuts, lime juice and lime peel until blended. Sprinkle with toasted coconut.

MAKES 6 TO 8 SERVINGS

WINTER SQUASH RISOTTO

2 tablespoons butter

1 tablespoon olive oil

1 large shallot or small onion, finely chopped

1½ cups uncooked arborio rice

1 teaspoon salt

½ teaspoon dried thyme

¼ teaspoon black pepper

¼ cup dry white wine

4 cups vegetable or chicken broth

2 cups cubed butternut squash (½-inch pieces)

½ grated Parmesan or Romano cheese, plus additional for garnish

1. Press Sauté; heat butter and oil in pot. Add shallot; cook and stir 2 minutes or until softened. Add rice; cook and stir 4 minutes or until rice is translucent. Stir in salt, thyme and pepper. Add wine; cook and stir about 1 minute or until evaporated. Add broth and squash; mix well.

2. Secure lid and move pressure release valve to sealing or locked position. Cook at high pressure 6 minutes.

3. When cooking is complete, press Cancel and use quick release.

4. Press Sauté; adjust heat to low. Cook risotto about 3 minutes or until desired consistency, stirring constantly. Stir in ½ cup cheese. Serve immediately with additional cheese.

MAKES 4 TO 6 SERVINGS

SWEET AND SOUR RED CABBAGE

2 slices thick-cut bacon, chopped

1 cup chopped onion

1 head red cabbage (2 pounds), thinly sliced (about 8 cups)

1 pound (about 2 medium) unpeeled Granny Smith apples, cut into ½-inch pieces

½ cup honey

½ cup cider vinegar

¼ cup plus 3 tablespoons water, divided

1 teaspoon salt

1 teaspoon celery salt

¼ teaspoon black pepper

2 tablespoons all-purpose flour

1. Press Sauté, cook bacon in pot until crisp. Remove to paper towel-lined plate.

2. Add onion to pot; cook and stir 3 minutes or until softened. Stir in cabbage, apples, honey, vinegar, ¼ cup water, salt, celery salt and pepper; mix well.

3. Secure lid and move pressure release valve to sealing or locked position. Cook at high pressure 5 minutes.

4. When cooking is complete, use natural release for 10 minutes, then release remaining pressure.

5. Stir remaining 3 tablespoons water into flour in small bowl until smooth. Press Sauté; add flour mixture to pot. Cook and stir about 3 minutes or until sauce thickens. Sprinkle with bacon; serve warm.

MAKES 8 SERVINGS

SPICY AFRICAN CHICKPEA AND SWEET POTATO STEW

Spice Paste (recipe follows)

1½ pounds sweet potatoes, peeled and cubed

1 can (about 15 ounces) chickpeas, rinsed and drained

1 can (about 14 ounces) diced tomatoes

1 package (10 ounces) frozen cut okra, thawed (about 2½ cups)

1 cup vegetable broth or water

Hot cooked couscous (optional)

Hot pepper sauce

Fresh cilantro sprigs (optional)

1. Prepare Spice Paste.

2. Combine sweet potatoes, chickpeas, tomatoes, okra, broth and Spice Paste in pot; mix well.

3. Secure lid and move pressure release valve to sealing or locked position. Cook at high pressure 3 minutes.

4. When cooking is complete, press Cancel and use quick release. Serve stew with couscous and hot pepper sauce, if desired. Garnish with cilantro.

MAKES 4 SERVINGS

SPICE PASTE: Combine 6 cloves peeled garlic and 1 teaspoon salt in small food processor or blender; process until garlic is finely chopped. Add 2 teaspoons paprika, 1½ teaspoons cumin seeds, 1 teaspoon black pepper, ½ teaspoon ground ginger and ½ teaspoon ground allspice; process 15 seconds. With motor running, pour 1 tablespoon olive oil through feed tube; process until mixture forms paste.

PENNE WITH RICOTTA, TOMATOES AND BASIL

2 cans (about 14 ounces each) diced tomatoes with basil, garlic and oregano

2½ cups water

3 teaspoons salt, divided

1 package (16 ounces) uncooked penne pasta

1 container (15 ounces) ricotta cheese

⅔ cup chopped fresh basil

¼ cup extra virgin olive oil

1 tablespoon balsamic vinegar

1 clove garlic, minced

¼ teaspoon black pepper

Grated Parmesan cheese

1. Combine tomatoes, water and 2 teaspoons salt in pot; mix well. Stir in pasta.

2. Secure lid and move pressure release valve to sealing or locked position. Cook at high pressure 5 minutes.

3. Meanwhile, combine ricotta, basil, oil, vinegar, garlic, remaining 1 teaspoon salt and pepper in medium bowl; mix well.

4. When cooking is complete, press Cancel and use quick release. Drain any remaining liquid in pot. Add ricotta mixture to pot; stir gently to coat. Sprinkle with Parmesan just before serving.

MAKES 4 SERVINGS

LEMON PARMESAN CAULIFLOWER

1 cup water

3 tablespoons chopped fresh parsley

½ teaspoon grated lemon peel

1 large head cauliflower
  (2 to 3 pounds), trimmed

1 tablespoon butter

3 cloves garlic, minced

2 tablespoons lemon juice

½ teaspoon salt

¼ cup grated Parmesan cheese

1. Pour water into pot; stir in parsley and lemon peel. Place rack in pot; place cauliflower on rack.

2. Secure lid and move pressure release valve to sealing or locked position. Cook at high pressure 3 minutes.

3. When cooking is complete, press Cancel and use quick release. Remove rack from pot; place cauliflower in large bowl. Reserve ½ cup cooking liquid; discard remaining liquid.

4. Press Sauté; melt butter in pot. Add garlic; cook and stir 1 minute or until fragrant. Add lemon juice, salt and reserved ½ cup cooking liquid; cook and stir until heated through.

5. Spoon lemon sauce over cauliflower; sprinkle with cheese. Cut into wedges to serve.

MAKES 6 SERVINGS

BLACK BEAN AND SWEET POTATO CHILI

- **1 tablespoon olive oil**
- **1 large onion, chopped**
- **4 teaspoons chili powder**
- **2 cloves garlic, minced**
- **1 teaspoon salt**
- **1 teaspoon chipotle chili powder**
- **½ teaspoon ground cumin**
- **2 cans (about 15 ounces each) black beans, rinsed and drained**
- **1 large sweet potato, peeled and cut into ½-inch pieces**
- **1 can (about 14 ounces) diced tomatoes**
- **1 can (about 14 ounces) crushed tomatoes**
- **1½ cups vegetable broth or water**
- **Optional toppings: sour cream, sliced green onions, shredded Cheddar cheese and/or tortilla chips**

1. Press Sauté; heat oil in pot. Add onion; cook and stir 3 minutes or until softened. Add chili powder, garlic, salt, chipotle chili powder and cumin; cook and stir 1 minute. Add beans, sweet potato, diced tomatoes, crushed tomatoes and broth; mix well.

2. Secure lid and move pressure release valve to sealing or locked position. Cook at high pressure 4 minutes.

3. When cooking is complete, press Cancel and use quick release.

4. Press Sauté; cook and stir 3 to 5 minutes or until chili thickens to desired consistency. Serve with desired toppings.

MAKES 6 SERVINGS

SPICY BACON CHEESE GRITS

6 slices bacon, chopped

1 large shallot or small onion, finely chopped

1 serrano or jalapeño pepper,* minced

3½ cups chicken broth

1 cup uncooked grits**

½ teaspoon salt

¼ teaspoon black pepper

1 cup (4 ounces) shredded Cheddar cheese

½ cup half-and-half

2 tablespoons finely chopped green onion

*Chile peppers can sting and irritate the skin, so wear rubber gloves when handling peppers and do not touch your eyes.

**Do not use instant grits.

1. Press Sauté; cook bacon in pot until crisp. Drain on paper towel-lined plate. Drain off all but 1 tablespoon drippings.

2. Add shallot and serrano pepper to pot; cook and stir 2 minutes or until shallot is lightly browned. Add broth, grits, salt and black pepper; cook and stir 1 minute.

3. Secure lid and move pressure release valve to sealing or locked position. Cook at high pressure 14 minutes.

4. When cooking is complete, use natural release for 10 minutes, then release remaining pressure.

5. Stir grits until smooth. Add cheese, half-and-half and half of bacon; stir until well blended. Sprinkle with green onion and remaining bacon.

MAKES 4 SERVINGS

BARLEY WITH CURRANTS AND PINE NUTS

2 tablespoons butter

1 onion, finely chopped

2 cups vegetable broth

1 cup uncooked pearl barley

½ cup currants

½ teaspoon salt

¼ teaspoon black pepper

2 ounces (about ½ cup) pine nuts, toasted*

To toast pine nuts, cook in small skillet over medium heat 3 minutes or until lightly browned, stirring frequently.

1. Press Sauté; melt butter in pot. Add onion; cook and stir 5 minutes or until tender. Stir in broth, barley, currants, salt and pepper; mix well.

2. Secure lid and move pressure release valve to sealing or locked position. Cook at high pressure 18 minutes.

3. When cooking is complete, use natural release for 10 minutes, then release remaining pressure.

4. Stir in pine nuts. Serve warm or at room temperature.

MAKES 4 TO 6 SERVINGS

MUSHROOM AND CHICKPEA RAGOÛT

1 cup dried chickpeas, soaked 8 hours or overnight

3 tablespoons extra virgin olive oil

8 ounces sliced cremini mushrooms

8 ounces shiitake mushrooms,* stemmed and thinly sliced

1 onion, chopped

4 cloves garlic, minced

½ cup Madeira wine

2 teaspoons salt

1 teaspoon dried rosemary

Black pepper

1 can (28 ounces) crushed tomatoes

1 cup water

1 can (6 ounces) tomato paste

Polenta (recipe follows)

Or substitute an additional 8 ounces of cremini mushrooms for the shiitake mushrooms.

1. Drain and rinse chickpeas. Press Sauté; heat oil in pot. Add mushrooms, onion and garlic; cook and stir 6 minutes or until mushrooms are browned. Add Madeira, salt and rosemary; cook and stir 1 to 2 minutes or until liquid is almost evaporated. Season with pepper. Stir in tomatoes, water, chickpeas and tomato paste; mix well.

2. Secure lid and move pressure release valve to sealing or locked position. Cook at high pressure 22 minutes.

3. When cooking is complete, use natural release for 10 minutes, then release remaining pressure. Meanwhile, prepare Polenta.

4. Stir ragoût; serve over Polenta.

MAKES 6 SERVINGS

POLENTA: Combine 2 cups milk, 2 cups water and ¼ teaspoon salt in large saucepan; bring to a boil over medium-high heat. Slowly whisk in 1 cup instant polenta in thin steady stream. Cook 4 to 5 minutes or until thick and creamy, whisking constantly. Remove from heat; stir in ½ cup grated Parmesan cheese.

BLACK AND WHITE CHILI

1 tablespoon vegetable oil

1 pound chicken tenders, cut into ¾-inch pieces

1 cup coarsely chopped onion

1 can (about 14 ounces) fire-roasted diced tomatoes

1 can (about 15 ounces) Great Northern beans, rinsed and drained

1 can (about 15 ounces) black beans, rinsed and drained

2 tablespoons chili seasoning mix

½ teaspoon salt

Hot pepper sauce (optional)

1. Press Sauté; heat oil in pot. Add chicken and onion; cook and stir 5 minutes or until chicken begins to brown. Stir in tomatoes; cook 1 minute, scraping up browned bits from bottom of pot. Stir in beans, chili seasoning mix and salt; mix well.

2. Secure lid and move pressure release valve to sealing or locked position. Cook at high pressure 5 minutes.

3. When cooking is complete, use natural release for 10 minutes, then release remaining pressure. Serve with hot pepper sauce, if desired.

MAKES 4 SERVINGS

SERVING SUGGESTION: Serve over hot cooked rice or pasta.

ASPARAGUS-PARMESAN RISOTTO

4 tablespoons (½ stick) butter, divided

1 tablespoon olive oil

1 onion, finely chopped

1½ cups uncooked arborio rice

1 teaspoon salt

¼ cup dry white wine

4 cups vegetable broth

2½ cups fresh asparagus pieces (about 1 inch)

⅔ cup frozen peas

1 cup grated Parmesan cheese

Shaved Parmesan cheese (optional)

1. Press Sauté; heat 3 tablespoons butter and oil in pot. Add onion; cook and stir 2 minutes or until softened. Add rice; cook and stir 2 minutes or until rice is translucent. Stir in salt. Add wine; cook and stir about 1 minute or until evaporated. Add broth; mix well.

2. Secure lid and move pressure release valve to sealing or locked position. Cook at high pressure 5 minutes.

3. When cooking is complete, press Cancel and use quick release. Stir in asparagus and peas. Secure lid and move pressure release valve to sealing or locked position. Cook at high pressure 1 minute.

4. When cooking is complete, press cancel and use quick release. Stir in remaining 1 tablespoon butter and 1 cup cheese. Serve immediately with additional cheese, if desired.

MAKES 4 TO 6 SERVINGS

ASPARAGUS-SPINACH RISOTTO: Substitute 1 cup baby spinach or chopped fresh spinach for peas. Proceed as directed.

ASPARAGUS-CHICKEN RISOTTO: Add 2 cups chopped or shredded cooked chicken to risotto with peas in step 3. Proceed as directed.

PASTA E CECI

1 cup dried chickpeas, soaked 8 hours or overnight

3 tablespoons olive oil

1 onion, chopped

1 carrot, chopped

2 teaspoons salt

1 clove garlic, minced

1 teaspoon minced fresh rosemary

1 can (28 ounces) whole tomatoes, undrained, crushed with hands or coarsely chopped

2 cups vegetable broth or water

1 bay leaf

⅛ teaspoon red pepper flakes

1 cup uncooked orecchiette pasta

Black pepper

Chopped fresh parsley (optional)

1. Drain and rinse chickpeas. Press Sauté; heat oil in pot. Add onion and carrot; cook and stir 8 minutes or until vegetables are softened. Add salt, garlic and rosemary; cook and stir 1 minute. Add chickpeas, tomatoes with liquid, broth, bay leaf and red pepper flakes; mix well.

2. Secure lid and move pressure release valve to sealing or locked position. Cook at high pressure 15 minutes.

3. When cooking is complete, use natural release for 5 minutes, then release remaining pressure.

4. Stir in pasta. Secure lid and move pressure release valve to sealing or locked position. Cook at high pressure 6 minutes.

5. When cooking is complete, press Cancel and use quick release. Remove and discard bay leaf. Season with black pepper; garnish with parsley.

MAKES 4 SERVINGS

TIP: To crush the tomatoes, take them out of the can one at a time and crush them between your fingers over the pot. Or coarsely chop them with with a knife.

RED BEANS AND RICE

1 **pound dried red kidney beans**

1 **tablespoon plus 1 teaspoon salt, divided**

2 **tablespoons olive oil**

2 **onions, chopped**

3 **stalks celery, chopped**

1 **green bell pepper, chopped**

4 **cloves garlic, minced**

1¾ **cups vegetable broth**

2 **teaspoons Italian seasoning**

1 **bay leaf**

½ **teaspoon liquid smoke**

½ **teaspoon black pepper**

¼ **teaspoon ground red pepper**

Hot cooked brown rice

Optional toppings: sliced cucumbers and carrots, sliced avocado, sliced green onions and hot pepper sauce

1. Place beans in large bowl; cover with water and stir in 1 tablespoon salt. Soak 8 hours or overnight.

2. Drain and rinse beans. Press Sauté; heat oil in pot. Add onions; cook and stir 5 minutes. Add celery, bell pepper, garlic and remaining 1 teaspoon salt; cook and stir 5 minutes or until vegetables are softened. Stir in broth, Italian seasoning, bay leaf, liquid smoke, black pepper and red pepper; mix well.

3. Secure lid and move pressure release valve to sealing or locked position. Cook at high pressure 12 minutes.

4. When cooking is complete, use natural release for 10 minutes, then release remaining pressure. Press Sauté; cook 3 to 5 minutes or until thickened, stirring frequently. For thicker beans, mash lightly with potato masher. Serve with rice and desired toppings.

MAKES 6 SERVINGS

FRUITY WHOLE-GRAIN CEREAL

2¼ cups water

¼ cup steel-cut oats

¼ cup uncooked pearl barley

¼ cup uncooked brown rice

½ teaspoon salt

½ cup milk

⅓ cup golden raisins

¼ cup finely chopped dried dates

¼ cup chopped dried plums

2 tablespoons packed brown sugar

½ teaspoon ground cinnamon

1. Combine water, oats, barley, rice and salt in pot; mix well.

2. Secure lid and move pressure release valve to sealing or locked position. Cook at high pressure 20 minutes.

3. When cooking is complete, use natural release for 10 minutes, then release remaining pressure.

4. Stir in milk, raisins, dates, dried plums, brown sugar and cinnamon; mix well. Serve hot. Refrigerate any leftover cereal in airtight container.

MAKES 4 TO 6 SERVINGS

TIP: To reheat cereal, place one serving in microwavable bowl. Microwave on HIGH 30 seconds; stir. Add water or milk to reach desired consistency. Microwave just until hot.

CHICKPEA TIKKA MASALA

1¼ **cups dried chickpeas, soaked 8 hours or overnight**

1 **tablespoon olive oil**

1 **onion, chopped**

3 **cloves garlic, minced**

1 **tablespoon minced fresh ginger or ginger paste**

1 **tablespoon garam masala**

1½ **teaspoons salt**

1 **teaspoon ground coriander**

1 **teaspoon ground cumin**

¼ **teaspoon ground red pepper**

1 **can (28 ounces) crushed tomatoes**

1 **can (about 13 ounces) coconut milk**

1 **package (about 12 ounces) paneer cheese, cut into 1-inch cubes**

Hot cooked brown basmati rice (optional)

Chopped fresh cilantro

1. Drain and rinse chickpeas. Press Sauté; heat oil in pot. Add onion; cook and stir 5 minutes or until translucent. Add garlic, ginger, garam masala, salt, coriander, cumin and red pepper; cook and stir 1 minute. Stir in chickpeas, tomatoes and coconut milk; mix well.

2. Secure lid and move pressure release valve to sealing or locked position. Cook at high pressure 22 minutes.

3. When cooking is complete, use natural release for 10 minutes, then release remaining pressure.

4. Press Sauté; adjust heat to low. Add paneer; stir gently. Cook 5 minutes or until paneer is heated through, stirring occasionally. Serve over rice, if desired; garnish with cilantro.

MAKES 4 SERVINGS

VARIATION: For a vegan dish, substitute one package (about 12 ounces) firm silken tofu, drained and cut into 1-inch cubes, for the paneer.

CHEESY POLENTA

5 cups vegetable broth

½ teaspoon salt

1½ cups uncooked instant polenta

½ cup grated Parmesan cheese, plus additional for serving

4 tablespoons (½ stick) butter, cubed

Fried sage leaves (optional)

1. Combine broth and salt in pot; slowly whisk in polenta until blended.

2. Secure lid and move pressure release valve to sealing or locked position. Cook at high pressure 5 minutes.

3. When cooking is complete, use natural release for 5 minutes, then release remaining pressure.

4. Whisk in ½ cup cheese and butter until well blended. (Polenta may appear separated immediately after cooking but will come together when stirred.) Serve with additional cheese; garnish with sage.

MAKES 6 SERVINGS

NOTE: Chicken broth may be substituted for vegetable broth. Or use water and add an additional ½ teaspoon salt when whisking in the polenta.

TIP: Spread any leftover polenta in a baking dish and refrigerate until cold. Cut the cold polenta into sticks or slices, brush with olive oil and pan-fry or grill until lightly browned.

FRIJOLES BORRACHOS (DRUNKEN BEANS)

1 pound dried pinto beans, soaked 8 hours or overnight

6 slices bacon, chopped

1 large onion, chopped

3 jalapeño peppers,* seeded and finely chopped

1 tablespoon minced garlic

1 tablespoon dried oregano

1 cup dark Mexican beer

1 can (about 14 ounces) diced tomatoes

1 cup water

¾ teaspoon salt

¼ cup chopped fresh cilantro

*Jalapeño peppers can sting and irritate the skin, so wear rubber gloves when handling peppers and do not touch your eyes.

1. Drain and rinse beans. Press Sauté; cook bacon in pot until crisp. Drain off all but 2 tablespoons drippings. Add onion to pot; cook and stir 3 minutes or until softened and lightly browned. Add jalapeños, garlic and oregano; cook and stir 1 minute. Stir in beer, scraping up browned bits from bottom of pot. Stir in beans, tomatoes, water and salt; mix well.

2. Secure lid and move pressure release valve to sealing or locked position. Cook at high pressure 22 minutes.

3. When cooking is complete, use natural release for 10 minutes, then release remaining pressure.

4. Press Sauté; cook 3 minutes, mashing beans slightly until broth is thickened and creamy. Stir in cilantro.

MAKES 6 TO 8 SERVINGS

ASIAN KALE
AND CHICKPEAS

2 cups dried chickpeas, soaked
8 hours or overnight

1 tablespoon plus 1 teaspoon sesame
oil, divided

1 medium onion, thinly sliced

2 teaspoons grated fresh ginger,
divided

2 cloves garlic, minced, divided

2 jalapeño peppers,* finely chopped,
divided

2 cups vegetable broth

½ cup water

1 teaspoon salt

8 cups loosely packed chopped kale
(about 1 bunch)

1 tablespoon lime juice

1 teaspoon grated lime peel

Hot cooked rice (optional)

*Jalapeño peppers can sting and irritate the skin,
so wear rubber gloves when handling peppers
and do not touch your eyes.

1. Drain and rinse chickpeas. Press Sauté; heat 1 tablespoon oil in pot. Add onion, 1 teaspoon ginger, 1 clove garlic and 1 jalapeño; cook and stir 3 minutes or until onion is softened. Stir in chickpeas, broth, water and salt; mix well.

2. Secure lid and move pressure release valve to sealing or locked position. Cook at high pressure 15 minutes.

3. When cooking is complete, use natural release for 10 minutes, then release remaining pressure. Stir in kale. Secure lid and move pressure release valve to sealing or locked position. Cook at high pressure 3 minutes.

4. When cooking is complete, press Cancel and use quick release.

5. If there is excess liquid in pot, press Sauté and cook 2 to 3 minutes or until liquid evaporates. Stir in remaining 1 teaspoon oil, 1 teaspoon ginger, 1 clove garlic, 1 jalapeño, lime juice and lime peel. Season with additional salt, if desired. Serve with rice, if desired.

MAKES 4 TO 6 SERVINGS

EASY DIRTY RICE

1½ **cups uncooked long grain rice**

8 **ounces bulk Italian sausage**

1½ **cups water**

1 **onion, finely chopped**

1 **green bell pepper, finely chopped**

½ **cup finely chopped celery**

1½ **teaspoons salt**

¼ **teaspoon black pepper**

¼ **teaspoon ground red pepper**

½ **cup chopped fresh parsley**

1. Rinse rice well; drain in fine-mesh strainer.

2. Press Sauté; cook sausage in pot 6 to 8 minutes or until browned, stirring to break up meat. Drain fat. Stir in rice, water, onion, bell pepper, celery, salt, black pepper and red pepper; mix well.

3. Secure lid and move pressure release valve to sealing or locked position. Cook at high pressure 4 minutes.

4. When cooking is complete, use natural release for 10 minutes, then release remaining pressure. Stir in parsley.

MAKES 4 TO 6 SERVINGS

FARRO RISOTTO WITH MUSHROOMS AND SPINACH

2 tablespoons olive oil, divided

1 onion, chopped

12 ounces cremini mushrooms, stems trimmed, quartered

1 teaspoon salt

¼ teaspoon black pepper

2 cloves garlic, minced

1 cup uncooked pearled farro

1 sprig fresh thyme

1½ cups vegetable or chicken broth

1 package (5 to 6 ounces) baby spinach

½ cup grated Parmesan cheese

1. Press Sauté; heat 1 tablespoon oil in pot. Add onion; cook and stir 5 minutes or until translucent. Add remaining 1 tablespoon oil, mushrooms, salt and pepper; cook about 8 minutes or until mushrooms have released their liquid and are browned, stirring occasionally. Add garlic; cook and stir 1 minute. Add farro and thyme; cook and stir 1 minute. Stir in broth; mix well.

2. Secure lid and move pressure release valve to sealing or locked position. Cook at high pressure 10 minutes.

3. When cooking is complete, use natural release for 10 minutes, then release remaining pressure. Remove and discard thyme sprig.

4. Stir in spinach and cheese until spinach is wilted.

MAKES 4 SERVINGS

LENTIL BOLOGNESE

2 tablespoons olive oil

1 onion, chopped

1 carrot, chopped

1 stalk celery, chopped

2 cloves garlic, minced

1 teaspoon salt

½ teaspoon dried oregano

Pinch red pepper flakes

3 tablespoons tomato paste

¼ cup dry white wine

3¼ cups water or vegetable broth

1 can (28 ounces) crushed tomatoes

1 can (about 14 ounces) diced tomatoes

1 cup dried lentils, rinsed

1 portobello mushroom, gills removed, finely chopped

2 cups uncooked whole wheat rotini pasta

1. Press Sauté; heat oil in pot. Add onion, carrot and celery; cook and stir 7 minutes or until onion is lightly browned and carrot is softened.

2. Stir in garlic, salt, oregano and red pepper flakes. Add tomato paste; cook and stir 1 minute. Add wine; cook and stir until absorbed. Stir in water, crushed tomatoes, diced tomatoes, lentils and mushroom; mix well.

3. Secure lid and move pressure release valve to sealing or locked position. Cook at high pressure 5 minutes.

4. When cooking is complete, press Cancel and use quick release.

5. Stir in pasta. Secure lid and move pressure release valve to sealing or locked position. Cook at high pressure 4 minutes. When cooking is complete, press Cancel and use quick release.

MAKES 6 SERVINGS

DESSERTS

CUSTARD BRÛLÉE

5 egg yolks
½ cup granulated sugar
¼ teaspoon salt
1 cup whipping cream
1 cup milk
1 teaspoon vanilla
¼ teaspoon ground cinnamon
Ground nutmeg (optional)
1¼ cups water
¼ cup packed brown sugar

1. Whisk egg yolks, granulated sugar and salt in medium bowl until blended. Add cream, milk and vanilla; whisk until well blended. Pour into 6- to 7-inch (1½-quart) soufflé dish or round casserole that fits inside pot. Sprinkle with cinnamon and nutmeg, if desired. Cover tightly with foil.

2. Pour water into pot. Place soufflé dish on rack; lower rack into pot.

3. Secure lid and move pressure release valve to sealing or locked position. Cook at high pressure 35 minutes.

4. When cooking is complete, press Cancel and use quick release.

5. Remove soufflé dish from pot. Remove foil; cool to room temperature. Cover and refrigerate 3 to 4 hours or until chilled.

6. Just before serving, preheat broiler. Sprinkle brown sugar evenly over top of custard. Broil 4 inches from heat 1 to 2 minutes or until sugar bubbles and browns.

MAKES 6 TO 8 SERVINGS

CHOCOLATE CHEESECAKE

22 chocolate crème-filled sandwich
cookies

¼ cup (½ stick) butter, melted

¼ cup seedless raspberry jam

3 tablespoons whipping cream

1 teaspoon instant coffee granules
or espresso powder (optional)

½ cup semisweet chocolate chips
or 3 ounces chopped bittersweet
chocolate

1½ packages (8 ounces each) cream
cheese, softened

½ cup sugar

2 eggs

½ teaspoon vanilla

1¼ cups water

Whipped cream and fresh
raspberries (optional)

1. Wrap outside of 7-inch springform pan with heavy-duty foil. Place cookies in food processor; process until finely ground. With motor running, drizzle in butter; process until well blended. Press mixture firmly onto bottom of prepared pan. Spread jam over crust. Refrigerate crust while preparing filling.

2. Heat cream and coffee granules, if desired, in small saucepan until bubbles form around edge of pan. Remove from heat; add chocolate and let stand 2 minutes. Stir until well blended and smooth. Cool slightly.

3. Beat cream cheese in large bowl with electric mixer at medium-high speed until smooth. Add sugar; beat until light and fluffy. Add eggs, one at a time, beating well after each addition. Add vanilla and melted chocolate mixture; beat at low speed just until blended. Spread in prepared crust. (Pan should not be filled higher than ½ inch from top.) Cover pan tightly with foil.

4. Pour water into pot. Place pan on rack; lower rack into pot. Secure lid and move pressure release valve to sealing or locked position. Cook at high pressure 45 minutes.

5. When cooking is complete, press Cancel and use quick release. Remove pan from pot. Remove foil; cool 1 hour. Run thin knife around edge of cheesecake to loosen (do not remove side of pan). Refrigerate 2 to 3 hours or overnight.

6. Remove side of pan. Garnish with whipped cream and raspberries.

MAKES 8 SERVINGS

POACHED AUTUMN FRUIT

1 **orange, peeled and halved**

2½ **to 3 cups water**

½ **cup dried cranberries**

¼ **cup sugar**

2 **tablespoons honey**

1 **teaspoon vanilla**

1 **whole cinnamon stick**

2 **Granny Smith apples, peeled and halved**

2 **Bartlett pears, peeled and quartered**
  Vanilla ice cream (optional)

1. Squeeze juice from orange halves into pot; place orange halves in pot. Add 2½ cups water, cranberries, sugar, honey, vanilla and cinnamon stick; mix well. Add apples and pears; stir to coat. (Liquid should just cover fruit; if fruit is not covered, add additional water to cover.)

2. Secure lid and move pressure release valve to sealing or locked position. Cook at high pressure 1 minute.

3. When cooking is complete, press Cancel and use quick release. Remove apples, pears and cranberries to plate; let stand until cool enough to handle.

4. Meanwhile, press Sauté; cook about 10 minutes or until liquid is reduced by one third and thickens slightly. Discard orange halves and cinnamon stick. Pour liquid through fine-mesh strainer into medium bowl; return to pot.

5. Cut apple and pears into 1-inch pieces. Add to pot; stir gently to coat. Serve with ice cream, if desired.

MAKES 4 TO 6 SERVINGS

PLUM BREAD PUDDING

6 cups cubed brioche, egg bread or challah (1-inch cubes)

1½ tablespoons butter

2 large plums, pitted and cut into thin wedges

⅓ cup plus ½ tablespoon sugar, divided

3 eggs

¾ cup half-and-half

½ cup milk

½ teaspoon vanilla

¼ teaspoon salt

¼ teaspoon ground cinnamon

1¼ cups water

Whipping cream or vanilla ice cream (optional)

1. Preheat oven to 400°F. Spray 6- to 7-inch (1½-quart) soufflé dish or round baking dish that fits inside pot with nonstick cooking spray.

2. Spread bread cubes in single layer on ungreased baking sheet. Bake 6 to 7 minutes or until lightly toasted, stirring halfway through baking time.

3. Meanwhile, melt butter in large skillet over medium-high heat. Add plums and ½ tablespoon sugar; cook 2 minutes or until plums are softened and release juices. Beat eggs in large bowl. Add half-and-half, milk, remaining ⅓ cup sugar, vanilla, salt and cinnamon; mix well. Add plums and toasted bread cubes; stir gently to coat. Pour into prepared soufflé dish. Cover dish tightly with foil.

4. Pour water into pot. Place soufflé dish on rack; lower rack into pot.

5. Secure lid and move pressure release valve to sealing or locked position. Cook at high pressure 35 minutes. When cooking is complete, use natural release for 10 minutes, then release remaining pressure.

6. Remove soufflé dish from pot. Let stand, covered, 15 minutes. Remove foil; serve warm with cream, if desired.

MAKES 6 SERVINGS

SOUTHERN SWEET POTATO CUSTARD

1 can (16 ounces) cut sweet potatoes, drained

1 can (12 ounces) evaporated milk, divided

½ cup packed brown sugar

2 eggs, lightly beaten

1 teaspoon ground cinnamon

½ teaspoon ground ginger

¼ teaspoon salt

1¼ cups water

Whipped cream (optional)

Ground nutmeg (optional)

1. Combine sweet potatoes and ¼ cup evaporated milk in food processor or blender; process until smooth. Add remaining milk, brown sugar, eggs, cinnamon, ginger and salt; process until well blended. Pour into 6- to 7-inch (1½-quart) soufflé dish or round baking dish that fits inside pot. Cover dish tightly with foil.

2. Pour water into pot. Place soufflé dish on rack; lower rack into pot.

3. Secure lid and move pressure release valve to sealing or locked position. Cook at high pressure 40 minutes.

4. When cooking is complete, use natural release for 10 minutes, then release remaining pressure. Uncover; let stand 30 minutes.

5. Remove soufflé dish from pot. Remove foil; cool 30 minutes. Garnish with whipped cream and nutmeg.

MAKES 4 SERVINGS

QUICK AND EASY KHEER (INDIAN RICE PUDDING)

3 cups whole milk

⅔ cup sugar

1 cup uncooked basmati rice, rinsed and drained

½ cup golden raisins

3 whole green cardamom pods *or* ¼ teaspoon ground cardamon

¼ teaspoon salt

Grated orange peel (optional)

Pistachio nuts (optional)

1. Combine milk and sugar in pot; stir until sugar is dissolved. Add rice, raisins, cardamom and salt; mix well.

2. Secure lid and move pressure release valve to sealing or locked position. Cook at high pressure 5 minutes.

3. When cooking is complete, use natural release for 10 minutes, then release remaining pressure.

4. Stir rice pudding well before serving. (Pudding will thicken upon standing.) Garnish with orange peel and pistachios.

MAKES 6 TO 8 SERVINGS

SUPERFAST APPLESAUCE

2 pounds (about 4 medium) sweet apples (such as Fuji, Gala or Honeycrisp), peeled and cut into 1-inch pieces

2 pounds (about 4 medium) Granny Smith apples, peeled and cut into 1-inch pieces

⅓ cup water

2 to 4 tablespoons packed brown sugar, divided

1 tablespoon lemon juice

1 teaspoon ground cinnamon

⅛ teaspoon salt

⅛ teaspoon ground nutmeg

⅛ teaspoon ground cloves

1. Combine apples, water, 2 tablespoons brown sugar, lemon juice, cinnamon, salt, nutmeg and cloves in pot; mix well.

2. Secure lid and move pressure release valve to sealing or locked position. Cook at high pressure 4 minutes.

3. When cooking is complete, press Cancel and use quick release.

4. Stir applesauce; taste for seasoning and add remaining 2 tablespoons brown sugar, if desired. If there is excess liquid in pot, press Sauté and cook 2 to 3 minutes or until liquid evaporates. Cool completely before serving.

MAKES 4 CUPS

PUMPKIN BREAD PUDDING

1 **cup whole milk**

2 **eggs**

½ **cup canned pumpkin**

⅓ **cup packed brown sugar**

1 **tablespoon butter, melted**

1½ **teaspoons ground cinnamon**

1 **teaspoon vanilla**

¼ **teaspoon salt**

¼ **teaspoon ground nutmeg**

8 **slices cinnamon raisin bread, torn into small pieces (about 4 cups)**

1¼ **cups water**

Bourbon Caramel Sauce (optional, recipe follows)

1. Spray 6- to 7-inch (1½-quart) soufflé dish or round baking dish that fits inside pot with nonstick cooking spray. Whisk milk, eggs, pumpkin, brown sugar, butter, cinnamon, vanilla, salt and nutmeg in large bowl until well blended. Add bread cubes; toss to coat. Pour into prepared dish; cover tightly with foil.

2. Pour water into pot. Place soufflé dish on rack; lower rack into pot.

3. Secure lid and move pressure release valve to sealing or locked position. Cook at high pressure 40 minutes.

4. When cooking is complete, use natural release for 10 minutes, then release remaining pressure.

5. Remove soufflé dish from pot. Remove foil; cool 15 minutes. Meanwhile, prepare Bourbon Caramel Sauce, if desired. Serve bread pudding warm with sauce.

MAKES 4 SERVINGS

BOURBON CARAMEL SAUCE: Combine ¼ cup (½ stick) butter, ¼ cup packed brown sugar and ¼ cup whipping cream in small saucepan; bring to a boil over high heat, stirring frequently. Remove from heat; stir in 1 tablespoon bourbon.

CHOCOLATE SURPRISE CRÈME BRÛLÉE

3 ounces bittersweet chocolate, finely chopped

5 egg yolks

1¾ cups whipping cream

½ cup granulated sugar

¼ teaspoon salt

1 teaspoon vanilla

1 cup water

¼ cup demerara or raw sugar

1. Spray bottoms of five 6-ounce ramekins or custard cups with nonstick cooking spray. Divide chocolate evenly among ramekins.

2. Whisk egg yolks in medium bowl. Combine cream, granulated sugar and salt in medium saucepan; bring to a simmer over medium heat. Slowly pour ¼ cup hot cream mixture into egg yolks, whisking until blended. Add remaining cream mixture in thin steady stream, whisking constantly. Pour through fine-mesh strainer into clean bowl. Stir in vanilla. Ladle custard mixture into prepared ramekins over chocolate. Cover each ramekin tightly with foil.

3. Pour water into pot; place rack in pot. Arrange ramekins on rack, stacking as necessary.

4. Secure lid and move pressure release valve to sealing or locked position. Cook at high pressure 6 minutes.

5. When cooking is complete, use natural release for 10 minutes, then release remaining pressure. Remove ramekins from pot; cool to room temperature. Refrigerate until ready to serve.

6. Just before serving, preheat broiler. Place ramekins on baking sheet; sprinkle tops of custards with demerara sugar. Broil 4 inches from heat 1 to 2 minutes or until sugar bubbles and browns.

MAKES 5 SERVINGS

ESPRESSO CRÈME BRÛLÉE: Reduce cream to 1½ cups and add ¼ cup espresso. Heat mixture in saucepan with sugar and salt as directed in step 2.

BRIOCHE RUM CUSTARD

1¾ **cups whipping cream**

2 **eggs**

⅓ **cup packed dark brown sugar**

3 **tablespoons light rum**

1 **teaspoon vanilla**

¼ **teaspoon salt**

1 **loaf (10 to 12 ounces) brioche bread or challah, torn into pieces**

½ **cup chopped pecans, divided**

1¼ **cups water**

Caramel or butterscotch ice cream topping (optional)

1. Spray 6- to 7-inch (1½-quart) soufflé dish or round baking dish that fits inside pot with nonstick cooking spray.

2. Whisk cream, eggs, brown sugar, rum, vanilla and salt in large bowl until well blended. Add brioche and ¼ cup pecans; stir until blended, Pour into prepared dish; sprinkle with remaining ¼ cup pecans. Cover dish tightly with foil.

3. Pour water into pot. Place soufflé dish on rack; lower rack into pot.

4. Secure lid and move pressure release valve to sealing or locked position. Cook at high pressure 35 minutes.

5. When cooking is complete, use natural release for 10 minutes, then release remaining pressure.

6. Remove soufflé dish from pot. Remove foil; serve warm or at room temperature. Drizzle with caramel topping, if desired.

MAKES 4 TO 6 SERVINGS

SPICED CHOCOLATE BREAD PUDDING

1½ **cups whipping cream**

4 **ounces unsweetened chocolate, coarsely chopped**

2 **eggs, beaten**

½ **cup sugar**

1 **teaspoon vanilla**

¾ **teaspoon ground cinnamon, plus additional for garnish**

½ **teaspoon ground allspice**

⅛ **teaspoon salt**

3 **cups cubed Hawaiian-style sweet bread, challah or brioche bread (½-inch cubes)**

½ **cup currants**

1¼ **cups water**

Whipped cream (optional)

1. Spray 6- to 7-inch (1½-quart) soufflé dish or round baking dish that fits inside pot with nonstick cooking spray. Heat cream to a simmer in medium saucepan over medium heat. Remove from heat. Add chocolate; stir until melted and smooth.

2. Beat eggs in large bowl. Add sugar, vanilla, ¾ teaspoon cinnamon, allspice and salt; mix well. Add chocolate mixture; stir until well blended. Add bread cubes and currants; stir gently to coat. Pour into prepared soufflé dish; smooth top. Cover tightly with foil.

3. Pour water into pot. Place soufflé dish on rack; lower rack into pot.

4. Secure lid and move pressure release valve to sealing or locked position. Cook at high pressure 35 minutes.

5. When cooking is complete, use natural release for 10 minutes, then release remaining pressure.

6. Remove soufflé dish from pot;. Remove foil; serve warm or at room temperature. Top with whipped cream and additional cinnamon, if desired.

MAKES 6 TO 8 SERVINGS

PRESSURE COOKING TIMES

Meat	MINUTES UNDER PRESSURE	PRESSURE	RELEASE
Beef, Bone-in Short Ribs	35 to 45	High	Natural
Beef, Brisket	60 to 75	High	Natural
Beef, Ground	8	High	Natural
Beef, Roast (round, rump or shoulder)	60 to 70	High	Natural
Beef, Stew Meat	20 to 25	High	Natural or Quick
Lamb, Chops	5 to 10	High	Quick
Lamb, Leg or Shanks	35 to 40	High	Natural
Lamb, Stew Meat	12 to 15	High	Quick
Pork, Baby Back Ribs	25 to 30	High	Natural
Pork, Chops	7 to 10	High	Quick
Pork, Ground	5	High	Quick
Pork, Loin	15 to 25	High	Natural
Pork, Shoulder or Butt	45 to 60	High	Natural
Pork, Stew Meat	15 to 20	High	Quick

Poultry

Poultry	MINUTES UNDER PRESSURE	PRESSURE	RELEASE
Chicken Breasts, Bone-in	7 to 10	High	Quick
Chicken Breasts, Boneless	5 to 8	High	Quick
Chicken Thigh, Bone-in	10 to 14	High	Natural
Chicken Thigh, Boneless	8 to 10	High	Natural
Chicken Wings	10 to 12	High	Quick
Chicken, Whole	22 to 26	High	Natural
Eggs, Hard-Cooked (3 to 12)	9	Low	Quick
Turkey Breast, Bone-in	25 to 30	High	Natural
Turkey Breast, Boneless	15 to 20	High	Natural
Turkey Legs	35 to 40	High	Natural
Turkey, Ground	8 to 10	High	Quick

Seafood

Seafood	MINUTES UNDER PRESSURE	PRESSURE	RELEASE
Cod	2 to 3	Low	Quick
Crab	2 to 3	Low	Quick
Halibut	6	Low	Quick
Mussels	1 to 2	Low	Quick
Salmon	4 to 5	Low	Quick
Scallops	1	Low	Quick
Shrimp	2 to 3	Low	Quick
Swordfish	4 to 5	Low	Quick
Tilapia	3	Low	Quick

Dried Beans and Legumes

	UNSOAKED	SOAKED	PRESSURE	RELEASE
Black Beans	22 to 25	8 to 10	High	Natural
Black-Eyed Peas	9 to 11	3 to 5	High	Natural
Cannellini Beans	30 to 35	8 to 10	High	Natural
Chickpeas	35 to 40	18 to 22	High	Natural
Great Northern Beans	25 to 30	7 to 10	High	Natural
Kidney Beans	20 to 25	8 to 12	High	Natural
Lentils, Brown or Green	10 to 12	n/a	High	Natural
Lentils, Red or Yellow Split	1	n/a	High	Natural
Navy Beans	20 to 25	7 to 8	High	Natural
Pinto Beans	22 to 25	8 to 10	High	Natural
Split Peas	8 to 10	n/a	High	Natural

Grains

	LIQUID PER CUP	MINUTES UNDER PRESSURE	PRESSURE	RELEASE
Barley, Pearled	2	18 to 22	High	Natural
Barley, Whole	2½	30 to 35	High	Natural
Bulgur	3	8	High	Natural
Farro	2	10 to 12	High	Natural
Grits, Medium	4	12 to 15	High	10 minute natural
Millet	1.5	1	High	Natural
Oats, Rolled	2	4 to 5	High	10 minute natural
Oats, Steel-Cut	3	10 to 13	High	10 minute natural
Quinoa	1½	1	High	10 minute natural
Polenta, Instant	3	5	High	5 minute natural
Rice, Arborio	2	6 to 7	High	Quick
Rice, Brown	1	22	High	10 minute natural
Rice, White Long Grain	1	4	High	10 minute natural

Vegetables	MINUTES UNDER PRESSURE	PRESSURE	RELEASE
Artichokes, Whole	9 to 12	High	Natural
Beets, Medium Whole	18 to 24	High	Quick
Brussels Sprouts, Whole	2 to 3	High	Quick
Cabbage, Sliced	3 to 5	High	Quick
Carrots, Sliced	2 to 4	High	Quick
Cauliflower, Florets	2 to 3	High	Quick
Cauliflower, Whole	3 to 5	High	Quick
Corn on the Cob	2 to 4	High	Quick
Eggplant	3 to 4	High	Quick
Fennel, Sliced	3 to 4	High	Quick
Green Beans	2 to 4	High	Quick
Kale	3	High	Quick
Leeks	3	High	Quick
Okra	3	High	Quick
Potatoes, Baby or Fingerling	6 to 10	High	Natural
Potatoes, New	7 to 9	High	Natural
Potatoes, 1-inch pieces	4 to 6	High	Quick
Potatoes, Sweet, 1-inch pieces	3	High	Quick
Potatoes, Sweet, Whole	8 to 12	High	Natural
Spinach	1	High	Quick
Squash, Acorn, Halved	7	High	Natural
Squash, Butternut, 1-inch pieces	4 to 6	High	Quick
Squash, Spaghetti, Halved	6 to 10	High	Natural
Tomatoes, cut into pieces for sauce	5	High	Natural

INDEX

METRIC CONVERSION CHART

VOLUME MEASUREMENTS (dry)

$^1/_8$ teaspoon = 0.5 mL
$^1/_4$ teaspoon = 1 mL
$^1/_2$ teaspoon = 2 mL
$^3/_4$ teaspoon = 4 mL
1 teaspoon = 5 mL
1 tablespoon = 15 mL
2 tablespoons = 30 mL
$^1/_4$ cup = 60 mL
$^1/_3$ cup = 75 mL
$^1/_2$ cup = 125 mL
$^2/_3$ cup = 150 mL
$^3/_4$ cup = 175 mL
1 cup = 250 mL
2 cups = 1 pint = 500 mL
3 cups = 750 mL
4 cups = 1 quart = 1 L

VOLUME MEASUREMENTS (fluid)

1 fluid ounce (2 tablespoons) = 30 mL
4 fluid ounces ($^1/_2$ cup) = 125 mL
8 fluid ounces (1 cup) = 250 mL
12 fluid ounces (1$^1/_2$ cups) = 375 mL
16 fluid ounces (2 cups) = 500 mL

WEIGHTS (mass)

$^1/_2$ ounce = 15 g
1 ounce = 30 g
3 ounces = 90 g
4 ounces = 120 g
8 ounces = 225 g
10 ounces = 285 g
12 ounces = 360 g
16 ounces = 1 pound = 450 g

DIMENSIONS

$^1/_{16}$ inch = 2 mm
$^1/_8$ inch = 3 mm
$^1/_4$ inch = 6 mm
$^1/_2$ inch = 1.5 cm
$^3/_4$ inch = 2 cm
1 inch = 2.5 cm

OVEN TEMPERATURES

250°F = 120°C
275°F = 140°C
300°F = 150°C
325°F = 160°C
350°F = 180°C
375°F = 190°C
400°F = 200°C
425°F = 220°C
450°F = 230°C

BAKING PAN SIZES

Utensil	Size in Inches/Quarts	Metric Volume	Size in Centimeters
Baking or Cake Pan (square or rectangular)	8×8×2	2 L	20×20×5
	9×9×2	2.5 L	23×23×5
	12×8×2	3 L	30×20×5
	13×9×2	3.5 L	33×23×5
Loaf Pan	8×4×3	1.5 L	20×10×7
	9×5×3	2 L	23×13×7
Round Layer Cake Pan	8×1½	1.2 L	20×4
	9×1½	1.5 L	23×4
Pie Plate	8×1¼	750 mL	20×3
	9×1¼	1 L	23×3
Baking Dish or Casserole	1 quart	1 L	—
	1½ quart	1.5 L	—
	2 quart	2 L	—